Sports Illustrated
BOARDSAILING

THE SPORTS ILLUSTRATED LIBRARY

BOOKS ON TEAM SPORTS

Baseball
Basketball
Pitching
Soccer

BOOKS ON INDIVIDUAL SPORTS

Bowling
Cross-Country Skiing
Golf
Racquetball
Tennis
Tumbling

Women's Gymnastics I:
    The Floor Exercise
    Event
Women's Gymnastics II:
    The Vaulting
    Balance Beam and
    Uneven Parallel Bars
    Events

BOOKS ON WATER SPORTS

Boardsailing
Canoeing
Scuba Diving

SPECIAL BOOKS

Backpacking

Sports Illustrated
BOARDSAILING

by MAJOR HALL

Photography by
Christopher Cunningham and Paul Kennedy

HARPER & ROW, PUBLISHERS, New York
Cambridge, Philadelphia, San Francisco, London
Mexico City, São Paulo, Sydney

1817

Pictures on pages 3, 12, 13, 14, 15, 18, 34, 88, 116, 126, 160, 180, 200, 206, 207, 210, 211, 213, by Paul Kennedy. All other photos by Christopher Cunningham.
Diagrams by Kim Llewellyn.

Special thanks to Island Windsurfing, 375 Thames Street, Newport, R.I.

Designer: C. Linda Dingler

Library of Congress Cataloging in Publication Data

Hall, Major.
  Sports illustrated boardsailing.

1. Windsurfing. I. Sports illustrated (Time, inc.)
II. Title. III. Title: Boardsailing.
GV811.63.W56H34 1985   797.1'72   82-48664
ISBN 0-06-015077-7
ISBN 0-06-091056-9 (pbk.)

85 86 87 88 10 9 8 7 6 5 4 3 2
85 86 87 88 10 9 8 7 6 5 4 3 2 1

Contents

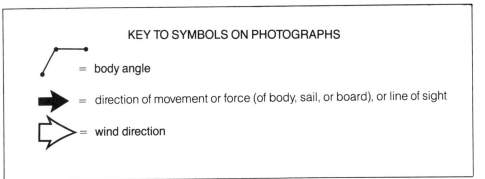

KEY TO SYMBOLS ON PHOTOGRAPHS

= body angle

= direction of movement or force (of body, sail, or board), or line of sight

= wind direction

1

Welcome to Boardsailing

If you're picking up this book because you've already tried boardsailing and want to learn more about it, then I know where you're coming from. I know the excitement and anticipation you are feeling, because I also felt them the first time I stepped on a board. And you know, six years later, after thousands of hours of boardsailing on all sorts of boards in different conditions all over the world, I still feel the same excitement and anticipation every time I step on a board.

But if you're picking up this book because you're just getting into boardsailing, let me warn you from the outset—boardsailing is addicting. Just ask any of the growing number of "addicts" of all shapes, sizes, and ages. They spend all summer on the water, don wet suits in the fall to extend the season, and then head south for vacations during the winter to get in a week or two of boardsailing in Florida, the Caribbean, or Mexico. I know, because I'm one of them. I think that boardsailing is the best thing to come along since sunshine and fresh air. I'm hooked. And to all of you who have just been hooked and all of you who are about to be, all I can say is, "Welcome to the world of boardsailing!" You'll be glad you entered it.

9

"Boardsailing is for everywhere and everyone." The author, practicing what he preaches, on Buzzards Bay, near Cape Cod.

People are usually surprised when they learn that boardsailing has been around for over fifteen years. The first sailboard was invented in Southern California in the mid-1960s by a surfing enthusiast named Hoyle Schweitzer and a sailing enthusiast named Jim Drake. Combining these two areas of interest, they put a surfboard together with a freesail system, which consisted of a mast, wishbone booms, and a sail attached to the board by a universal joint, allowing the entire rig to rotate 360 degrees or to be tilted in any direction. Logically, the craft was called a windsurfer and was sailed standing up, with the sailor supporting the rig by holding onto the wishbone booms (so named because of their oblong shape), trimming by rotating the rig, and steering by tilting the sail forward or back.

In the early years, the windsurfer was looked upon primarily as a toy or novelty item. No one was quite sure where it fit into the existing water sports scene. To sailors and surfers alike it was viewed as too radical, too untraditional. However, Schweitzer had enough foresight and faith in his invention to patent it and to begin manufacturing it under the brand name Windsurfer. Thus the sport was first known as *windsurfing.*

It wasn't until 1973, when the Windsurfer® and windsurfing were first introduced to Europe, that the sport began to take off. Immediately, the European ski industry adopted windsurfing as a summertime activity for skiers, ski instructors, and ski shops. In the next ten years, over 600,000 Scandinavians, French, Germans, Italians, Swiss, Dutch, and Austrians took up the sport. It spread like wildfire. Windsurfing resorts began to open. Windsurfing fashion lines appeared. There were windsurfing schools, windsurfing tours, windsurfing magazines, and windsurfing discos. It became the *in* thing to do.

During this period of tremendous growth, over 100 new board manufacturers entered the European market. Some of these were licensed by Hoyle Schweitzer, but many were not. This set off five years of complicated patent suits and countersuits, many of which are still tied up in the courts and unresolved today. But one significant result was that the name of the sport evolved from *windsurfing* to *boardsailing,* and the surfboard with a sail became a *sailboard,* since Schweitzer did not want his registered trademark of Windsurfer to become confused with a generic term.

Here in North America the Windsurfer® is still by far the largest class of sailboard, and many newcomers still refer to the sport as windsurfing. But now the sport that started in Southern California and spread to Europe is being imported back into the U.S. Many of the successful European board manufacturers, such as Bic, Mistral, Crit, HiFly, Magnum, Wayler, and Windglider, have entered the U.S. market and set off the beginnings of the boardsailing boom that we are experiencing now. Boardsailing has developed more slowly in the U.S. and Canada than in Europe, but we're catching up, and there is every indication that the growth of boardsailing in North America will eventually surpass its European counterpart.

Internationally, boardsailing has grown out of its outcast role and has become an accepted part of the yachting world. Seven or eight boardsailing classes hold annual world championships, with four of these recognized by the International Yacht Racing Union. There are even major professional boardsailing events being held in Europe, California, Hawaii, Japan, and Australia. But most significant is the fact that boardsailing has been selected as a new Olympic event, one of only a few new events to be added in many years.

Even television has discovered boardsailing. Not only are sailboards used in a number of commercials for everything from soft drinks to oil companies, but also some of the major championships are now being televised. In Europe it is not uncommon to find two or three networks covering an important competition live, with on-the-water cameras, interviews, and commentators. People have always said that watching sailing is as exciting as watching grass grow, but that doesn't apply to boardsailing.

WHY PEOPLE BOARDSAIL

Boardsailing is a truly unique activity. On the one hand, it is a combination of many popular recreational and competitive sports. But on the other hand, it is so new and different that it is like nothing else in existence.

Boardsailing has the freedom of sailing, the speed and excitement of skiing and surfing, the beauty of gymnastics, the grace of figure skating, and the free-flight sensation of sky diving and hang gliding. However, unlike these sports, boardsailing is not expensive, it is not restricted to a limited number of good sites, it is not susceptible to overcrowding, it does not require a lot of maintenance or preparation time and effort, it doesn't take tremendous strength or exceptional agility, and it is not dangerous.

What Is Boardsailing?

It's one of the fastest-growing, most social sports around, with boardsailors of all ages congregating on lakes, ponds, oceans—wherever a good breeze and a body of water can be found.

Boardsailing can be a relaxing solo passage across a tranquil mountain lake . . .

. . . or a healthy workout on a windswept coastal bay.

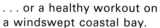

Families are boardsailing. Kids and grand-parents take to this sport just as fast as the family dog . . .

. . . and for boardsailors of all skill levels, there are regattas to satisfy that competitive urge.

For the freestyler, boardsailing is performing a split while "railriding" on the board's edge . . .

. . . while for the wave sailor, it's shooting off a big roller or zipping across the water's surface at speeds of up to 28 miles per hour.

No matter who you are or how limited your boardsailing skills, the pleasure of meeting the elements and of holding the wind in your hands is irresistible.

Boardsailing is a social sport, shared by friends and family. People can drop their sails in almost any conditions and sit on their boards and hold a conversation without quickly drifting apart or having to yell over the din of flapping sails. Or if it's an escape to peace and solitude you seek, you can sail off alone to enjoy a sunrise or a sunset or just a quiet moment. You can take a relaxing sail in a gentle breeze or get a good workout in a hard blow. It's athletic. It's aesthetic. It can be a pastime or a passion. Boardsailing is a sport for the body and the mind, the heart and the soul.

Boardsailing is for everyone, men and women, young and old, large and small. It's for the beginner, the intermediate, and the expert. It's for the racer, competing around an Olympic triangle, through a slalom course, or in a long distance race, against a group of friends at a local regatta or against the best in the world at an international championship. It's for the freestyle sailor, showing off for the sunbathers at the beach or going through a polished routine for the judges. It's for the wave sailor, riding and jumping the big break in Hawaii or carving high-speed turns and catching air off the chop on a windy midwestern lake. It's for passage makers, crossing San Francisco Bay, the Molikai Channel, the Atlantic Ocean or the neighborhood pond. It's for anyone who just likes to get out on the water and sail.

Boardsailing is for inland lakes or open oceans, light winds or strong, flat waters or waves. It's for Fort Lauderdale, Florida; Bar Harbor, Maine; Wichita, Kansas; Tucson, Arizona; Lake Tahoe, California; and Diamond Head, Hawaii. It's for Canada and the Caribbean. It's for home and away. Boardsailing is for everywhere and everyone.

LEARNING TO BOARDSAIL

"It looks awfully difficult to learn," you might say. But it's not. In fact, under the correct conditions, most people learn with less than five hours of practice. It doesn't take much strength. Good technique is far more important, which is one reason so many women become good boardsailors. If you can ski or skate or even ride a bicycle, you can learn to boardsail.

It's true that you spend a lot of time in the water when first learning, but then, so does everybody. Even the best boardsailors in the world started out falling as much as the next guy. It's kind of an initiation that everyone goes through. We make mistakes and get laughed at when we learn, and we get to laugh at others' mistakes when they learn. It's part of the fun, something that all boardsailors share. To this day I have boardsailing friends who remind me that when I was first learning, my stance looked something like a duck trying to lay an egg.

"But I don't know anything about sailing," you could protest. It doesn't matter. There are hundreds of thousands of examples of nonsailors, even relatively nonathletic people, who have mastered boardsailing. Because the board and rig are more like extensions of your body than is the case with a sailboat, you learn to sail almost instinctively. You don't have to know all the names of everything and how it all works to learn to boardsail. You just do it. Even the experienced sailor has to start at the beginning, just like everyone else. In fact, he needs to be careful not to let his knowledge of sailing get in the way of learning to boardsail.

Whether you are a sailor or not, one of the most important factors in determining how easily and quickly you learn to boardsail is the manner in which you approach it. This book has been designed to create in print the one-on-one teaching relationship that exists between an instructor and a student on the water. Don't be merely a passive reader of information. Be an active, involved learner. While you are reading, think of yourself as listening to an instructor who knows from experience how people best learn to boardsail, what problems they face, what particular skills and knowledge they need, and what they should be concentrating on.

Concentration is the key. To maintain a high level of concentration, think about and visualize exactly what you're going to do before you do it. For instance, if you are about to trim the sail and start sailing for the first time, picture in your mind what you want to do with your body. Think about what you've read, what the photos showed. Actually see yourself trimming the sail and sailing, not from a distance, but up close and in detail—where you put your feet, where you put your hands, the exact timing and position of what you do with the board, the rig, and your body. It's a bit like a mental dress rehearsal. You are actually practicing and learning the maneuver while you are visualiz-

A boardsailing lesson from a qualified instructor is a quick way to pick up basic technique. Note the tether in the left foreground which prevents the board from drifting too far from shore.

ing it. And afterward, this same process will help you to review what you did right and wrong.

Obviously, any form of distraction will make learning that much more difficult. Thus, in the following chapters I have carefully set up learning situations and sequences that eliminate as much as possible any variables not directly related to the particular skills being learned. These distractions might take the form of inappropriate weather conditions, a poor sailing location, or inadequate equipment. But perhaps the greatest distractions to learning are those that come from within.

Fear of failure is a common problem that can prevent people from learning, when they are actually fully capable of it. The best way to overcome this problem is simply by ignoring the end product and concentrating on the learning process. Worrying over whether you will succeed or not will not help you learn. Instead, keep a positive attitude, trust in yourself and this book's ability to teach, have fun, and remember that anyone can learn to boardsail so long as he or she doesn't mind getting wet. A positive attitude alone will not turn you into an accomplished boardsailor, but it will clear your mind of a large distraction and allow you to concentrate on the task at hand.

Another common learning problem is impatience. It is only natural to watch advanced boardsailors out jumping waves, blasting around in small gales, doing reverse railrides, and racing full displacement boards and to want to do the same. But you have to take it one step at a time. Improvement comes only through practice and time on the board. To go out in conditions you can't handle or to try things you're not yet ready for is not only frustrating, but also potentially dangerous. The learning progression in this book has been carefully designed to build one set of skills on top of another. To skip a learning stage, no matter how eager you are, will only make it that much more difficult to learn in the end. If you concentrate on the development of the necessary skills at each level, you will be surprised how quickly you progress.

One final learning tip: work with a friend. By taking turns watching each other, you'll each have someone spotting mistakes that you might not realize you're making, and at the same time profit from watching someone else's mistakes. *You should never sail alone when you are first learning—or even when you're beyond the learning stage, in certain places and conditions.*

Learning is fun—the challenge, the sense of accomplishment, even the falls. There is a unique thrill derived from learning to do something completely new and different. Don't treat the experience merely as a means to an end. Learning to boardsail is a tremendous source of enjoyment, excitement, and satisfaction in itself.

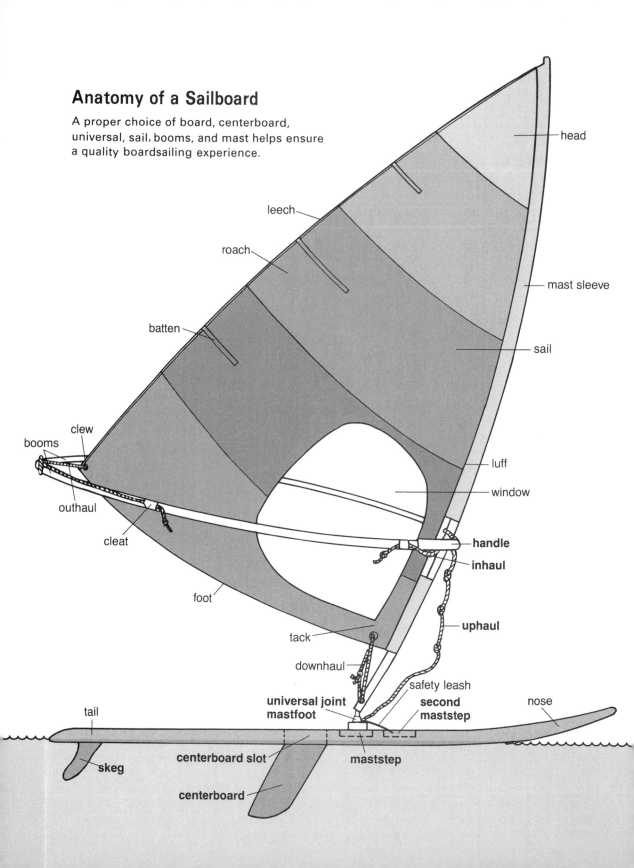

Anatomy of a Sailboard

A proper choice of board, centerboard, universal, sail, booms, and mast helps ensure a quality boardsailing experience.

head

leech

roach

mast sleeve

batten

sail

clew

booms

outhaul

luff

window

cleat

handle

inhaul

foot

uphaul

tack

downhaul

safety leash

universal joint
mastfoot

second
maststep

nose

tail

skeg

centerboard slot

maststep

centerboard

2

Equipment

The proper selection of equipment is important to any athlete in any sport, be it competitive or recreational. For the novice and the expert alike, performance depends greatly on whether one's equipment suits one's needs. For the beginning boardsailor, this selection process is even more critical, since an incorrect choice of board, sails, and other equipment can be a formidable obstacle to learning and in some cases even a threat to safety.

BOARD SELECTION

The primary characteristic of a good board to learn on is stability. Learning to balance can be enough of a challenge without also having to deal with a board that is so short or narrow that it is inherently unstable. Most learners should look for a board that is approximately 12½ feet long and about 26 inches wide, and that weighs around 45 pounds. A board with these rough dimensions should provide the average novice boardsailor of 100 to 160 pounds with enough buoyancy for a stable learning platform. If the board is significantly shorter or narrower or lighter, it will float

Sailboards come in a variety of sizes and shapes. The two boards in the center are good all-round recreational boards because they are wide enough and long enough to afford stability, but still provide good performance. The board on the left is an extra-wide learning board that provides increased stability, but little performance or challenge as the boardsailor progresses. The board on the right is strictly a racing board—long, narrow, and fast, but extremely unstable. In the background is a highwind board which is very fast and maneuverable in strong winds, but lacks adequate buoyancy to be suitable for the novice or in light or moderate winds.

lower in the water and be more difficult to balance on.

For someone over 160 pounds, it may be necessary to look into a board that is larger and more buoyant to support the additional weight. Similarly, someone under 100 pounds might do better with a smaller board that is easier to manage. Length, width, and weight provide a good guideline for board selection, but the best method for deciding if a board is buoyant enough for you is simply to stand on it in the water. If the rail sinks more than halfway below the surface, then there is not enough buoyancy for your weight. On the other hand, if stepping forward or back does not appreciably sink the nose or the tail, then there is a good chance that the board is too large and buoyant for your weight. If you are uncertain, it is better to have a board that is too buoyant than one that is not buoyant enough.

Another important characteristic that contributes greatly to the amount of stability in a board is the shape of the bottom. The flatter the bottom, the more stable the board. Round bottoms make very good racing boards, but they are generally far too difficult to stand on to serve as learning boards. In fact,

A   B   C

The flatter the bottom of a board, the more stable it will be. On these three boards, A is flat in the nose, B is V-shaped, and C is round.

trying to stand on a Division II Open Class racing board is like trying to survive a logrolling contest. This isn't to say that there aren't suitable learning boards with a certain amount of roundness toward the nose. The difference is that these boards are flat in back of the maststep where the sailor stands, whereas the all-out racing boards are round all the way back to the tail.

There are some boards available that have been designed specifically for learning. These are usually very wide, as much as 6 inches wider than the average board, which gives them both increased buoyancy and stability. All of these boards have flat bottoms, and some are even concave, which puts more buoyancy out by the rails and affords the greatest resistance to tipping. If you can borrow one of these boards, you will probably be able to learn quicker and more easily. However, if you are thinking about buying a specialized learning board, keep in mind that once you advance beyond the learning stage, you will probably outgrow the board. It is usually better to buy a board that will provide a compromise between stability and performance. It may not be quite as easy to learn on, but it will continue to be exciting and challenging as you become

Looking at the tails of the same three boards, A is flat, B is slightly rounded, and C is very round. Thus, A is the most stable, B is less stable, and C is the least stable.

A   B   C

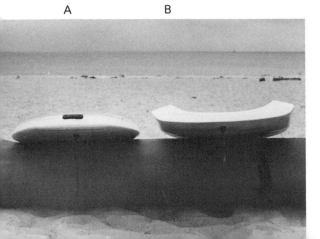
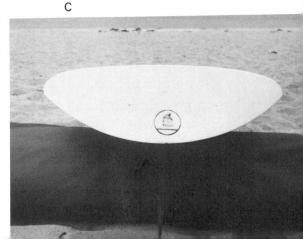

The convex deck (left) is the best shape for good footing. A concave deck (right) is not an ideal shape for good footing, but if the deck is hollow only at the tail and not forward where the sailor stands, it presents no problems.

a better boardsailor. In other words, practically and economically speaking, a good learning board should also be able to serve as a good intermediate board.

Almost all boards can be divided into three basic construction types: (1) polyethylene, (2) ABS plastic, and (3) fiberglass. Each of these materials has its own advantages and drawbacks, but for the learner, polyethylene and ABS boards are the most suitable. This is because they are softer and more forgiving than fiberglass boards. Not only are they less likely to develop cracks or holes through hard use or contact, but they also are less likely to cause injury if someone happens to fall on or against them. On the other hand, fiberglass boards are stiffer, give higher performance, and are easier to repair if they do get dinged. Polyethylene is at the other extreme, while ABS is a compromise between the two.

Deck design also should be considered when selecting a board. A flat, simple, clutter-free deck makes the best platform on which to learn. A slightly convex deck can be okay, but a concave deck definitely makes it more difficult for the beginner to learn how to balance and move. However, if only the nose or the tail of a board is hollowed and the deck area where the sailor stands is flat, there should be no impairment to learning. Regardless, a board should not have any sharp edges or protrusions to trip on or fall against.

A second deck consideration is the type and amount of nonskid surface. Here a compromise must be struck between a surface that is rough enough to provide a good grip for the feet, but not so rough that the deck is dangerous to fall against. If your polyethylene or ABS board does not have enough nonskid for your needs or if it begins to wear down with time and use, you can rough it up again with a wood rasp. This usually isn't a problem with fiberglass, since a durable, nonskid pattern is usually molded right into the deck. Just remember when you are checking nonskid on boards in the showroom that it will be wet most of the time you are using it. It's surprising how some deck surfaces can provide excellent traction on dry land, but be as slippery as a wet linoleum floor out on the water.

The Centerboard

The main purpose of a centerboard is to keep your sailboard from slipping sideways through the water, but it also adds a certain amount of stability. Thus, a longer centerboard can provide increased stability. However, there is a point where a centerboard gets so long that it is inconvenient to handle and actually adds to instability at high speeds. There are three basic types of centerboards. The most common type is the *kickup centerboard,* which can be pivoted up and back from its full down position. This makes it very convenient when sailing in or out of a shallow launching area or when trying to gain more control in heavy air. The only drawback with the kickup centerboard is that there is always a portion of it sticking up above deck level in the centerboard slot, to trip over or fall against.

The *daggerboard,* on the other hand, drops straight into the centerboard

The three types of centerboards. Kickups *(A,B)* pivot for limited adjustability; dagger boards *(C,D)* lift straight up or down only; fully retractable centerboards *(E)* pivot all the way up into the bottom of the board for full adjustability.

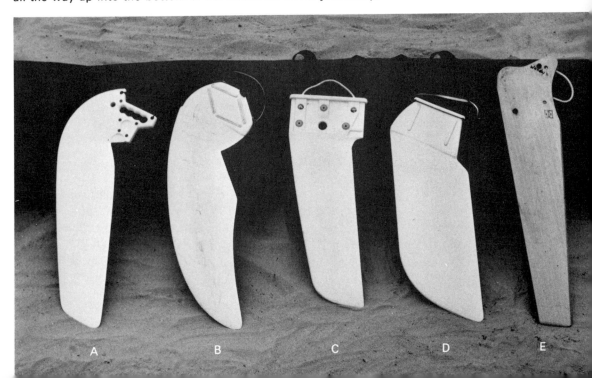

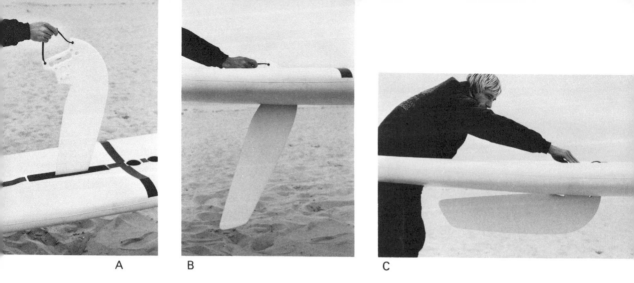

A B C

A kickup centerboard drops into place in the centerboard slot *(A)*, and can be fully lowered *(B)* or "kicked up" *(C)*, depending on water depth and wind and wave conditions.

slot so that it sits flush with the deck. However, the daggerboard can only be carried in a single, fixed, down position. It cannot be adjusted forward or back and must be completely removed from the slot in shallow water or to increase high-speed stability. And if by chance you hit bottom or some submerged object while the daggerboard is down, the damage to the board can be considerable.

The third type is the *fully retractable centerboard,* which is like a kickup centerboard, except that it pivots all the way up into the board, thus providing a wider range of adjustments. Generally, this type of centerboard arrangement has been more expensive than the other two and has therefore usually been reserved for the high-performance racing board. But recently, some popular recreational boards have come out with fully retractable centerboards. So if you don't mind the extra cost, you can get a centerboard system on your learning board that will afford you high performance adjustability when you reach a more advanced level of boardsailing.

The Universal

A good universal, which is the key connector between the board and the rig (consisting of mast, sail, and boom), must do four very important things: it must move freely in all directions; it must attach easily to the board; it must stay attached when you want it to; and it must detach when you want it to. One of the most frustrating occurrences in boardsailing is to have the universal pop

The top of the universal fits into the mast, while the bottom fits into a hole in the board forward of the centerboard slot. On this universal a rubber hourglass piece allows the mast and rig to move independently. An expandable rubber piece at the bottom keeps the system securely attached to the board. The safety leash, which prevents the rig from completely separating from the board if the universal pops out, is a boardsailor's single most important piece of safety equipment.

A pressure/friction universal system with a T -shaped base that fits into the board. The rubber collar covers a mechanical joint that permits the rig to pivot 360 degrees.

This variation of a pressure/friction universal system uses a piece of shockcord to help achieve a tighter fit in the board.

A two-pronged metal pin secures the base of this universal in the board. Under extreme pressure the pin bends, releasing the rig in emergency situations.

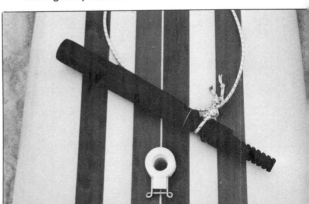

out of the board every time you try to pull the rig out of the water. On the other hand, it can be even worse when the universal doesn't pop out if you happen to get an arm or a leg caught between the mast and the board.

By far the most popular and potentially effective means of attaching the universal to the board is a mechanical, expandable system. This system has a mechanism by which a grip at the top of the connector is twisted to make the bottom of the unit expand and fit tighter in the hole. Thus the unit can be put in easily and tightened just enough so it will stay in during normal use but will release under a certain amount of pressure, like a ski binding. Then, after use, it is loosened to pull out again. The only problem with this system is that the mechanical parts are often susceptible to failure, especially if they are not kept clean of sand and salt.

The most straightforward system is the pressure/friction system, which works on the simple principle of a very tight fit. There are no mechanical parts to fail, but the connector piece on the universal and the corresponding hole in the board can both wear down and require layers of tape to maintain the necessary tight fit. And then, when the fit is tight enough, it usually takes some effort to put the connector in and take it out. The O-ring system works on a similar principle, with the rings forming a kind of suction seal in the hole. It also has problems staying in place, especially as the rubber rings wear down quickly. Furthermore, it is difficult to tape an O-ring connector so that it will fit tighter.

Although all three systems have their strengths and weaknesses, technology is providing better and more durable mechanical systems each year. Just keep in mind that there are some poorly designed and constructed mechanical systems as well. Before you buy anything, be sure to test it wet.

Sail and Rig Selection

Sail selection for the learner is important in that too large a sail can overpower you to the point where you are constantly pulled into the water, while too small a sail will not offer any aid to balance or provide enough power to maneuver. Most recreational boards come equipped with a *full-size sail* that runs approximately 60 square feet. This sail can be suitable for learning, but usually only in light winds or for fairly large people.

The average learner needs a smaller sail, one that allows him to go out in over 4 knots of wind without being overpowered. Probably the best sail for these

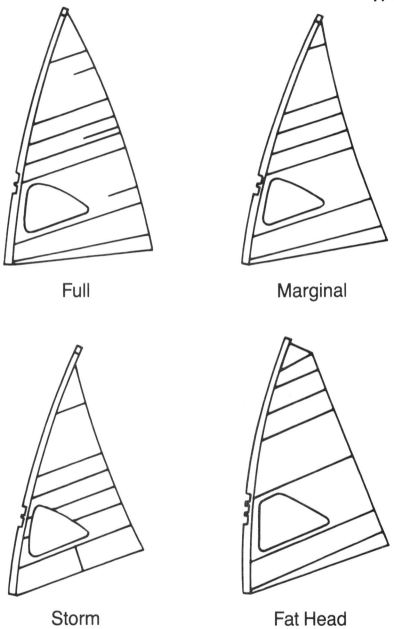

Full

Marginal

Storm

Fat Head

Choose sails according to the conditions you will be sailing in and your skill level.

needs is the *marginal sail,* which is approximately 50 square feet and can be handled by most novices in up to 8 knots of wind. Another nice thing about the marginal sail is that it continues to be a useful piece of equipment after you advance beyond the learning stage. Even as you get better and can sail in stronger winds, there will always be conditions that you cannot yet handle with a full-size sail. But with a marginal sail, you can get out and have fun and learn on days when you might otherwise have to sit on the beach and watch.

If you really want to extend the range of winds you can sail in, there is also the *storm sail,* which is even smaller than a marginal. At only about 40 square feet, it is a useful learning tool for very small persons or in areas where the prevailing wind strength is over 8 knots. Because of its size, the storm sail is a fairly specialized sail. For the average beginner in light conditions, it simply does not provide enough power so that one can learn proper sail-trim and board-handling techniques. And even as a recreational sail for more advanced, heavy-air use, the wind has to be blowing harder than what you are normally able to handle before the storm sail will provide any real challenge or performance.

The most important thing to look for in a rig is mast and booms that aren't too heavy, since you will be pulling them out of the water a lot in the beginning. The mast, which supports the sail, should be fiberglass, which is much more durable and forgiving than the aluminum masts used for high-performance racing. Booms, which you'll hold to support the rig and steer the board, can be either round or oval, depending on what feels most comfortable in your hands. The three main requirements for a good set of booms are the ability to achieve a tight connection at the mast with the inhaul line, outhaul-line cleats that won't slip, and a coating that provides a sure, comfortable grip.

In this last category, you are dealing with trade-offs similar to nonskid on the deck. You want a coating that will not slip in your hands, but not one so rough that it causes blisters. And again, when testing booms, remember that what grips well on dry land may not do so when it is wet. Also, check to see that the coating is durable and won't twist or slip on the booms. The boom coating is where your body connects to the rig, just as the nonskid is where your body connects to the board. This means that there is a lot of wear at these points. It also means that the comfort and efficiency of these connecting points greatly determine boardsailing performance.

SELECTING CLOTHING

On the one hand, the nice thing about getting dressed to boardsail is that most of the time you can get by with just a bathing suit. But on the other hand, there are some clothing items that can make boardsailing more comfortable and more enjoyable. Wet suit design and technology have come a long way from the heavy, restrictive suits developed for underwater diving. Today's wet suits are light, flexible, durable, and even stylish. They can extend the boardsailor's season and allow him to perform up to his abilities in a wider range of wind and weather conditions.

In certain areas where the water is relatively cold even in the middle of the summer, a wet suit is a must for the learner. It is impossible to concentrate on learning when you are constantly worried about a cold dunking. Nor is standing on the board shivering conducive to developing proper technique. Even in warmer areas, you start out spending a disproportionate amount of time in the water. A wet suit may not be essential for the average beginner, but it can make the learning experience easier, more pleasant, and, because it offers some protection when falling and climbing back on the board, safer.

There are many different wet suit styles designed for different boardsailing conditions and needs. The one most useful to the novice and learner is the *farmer john*. This one-piece suit covers just the legs and torso, protecting most of the body, while not getting you too hot or restricting shoulder and arm movement. Another useful style is a neoprene jacket with waterproof fabric sleeves. This keeps the torso warm and offers some protection to the arms and shoulders, but still leaves upper body movement unrestricted. These two suits —the farmer john and the jacket—are your best bargains because they are such a versatile combination. Each can be worn alone, depending on the conditions, or they can be worn together for maximum warmth. It's like getting three suits for the price of two.

There are many other styles available—vests, shorties, one-piece suits— but they are for more specialized use and aren't necessary items for the beginning boardsailor. Wet suits are also made out of a variety of materials. The warmest and least expensive suits are made out of plain neoprene, but you are better off paying extra to get a nylon-covered or lycra-covered neoprene suit that is still relatively warm, but is also far more resistent to wear and tear.

Clothing

A

B

The only other clothing item that the learner might consider is a pair of shoes. There are several different boardsailing shoes out on the market, ranging from inexpensive rubber slippers to some very expensive shoes and boots that will keep your feet warm in wet-suit conditions. But for learning, all you need is a pair of tennis shoes that will protect your feet and add a little extra traction. Just make sure that any shoe you use has as thin and flexible a sole as possible, since you want to get as close to the same feel for the board as you would with bare feet.

(A) A neoprene jacket with waterproof fabric sleeves (left), and a farmer john (center), alone or in combination (right) can make getting wet a whole lot more comfortable. (B) Vests (left), shorties (center), and one-piece suits (right) are designed to meet more specialized boardsailing needs.

Preparing to Sail

I know from experience the tremendous desire to get out on the water as soon as possible, to drive straight from the shop to the shore and get boardsailing. But in the best interests of life, limb, and learning, there are some very important preparation stages that must come between selecting your equipment and actually beginning to boardsail. To get out on the water too soon, before fully understanding what you are getting into, will just inhibit learning. Plus, a little advance planning and shoreside learning will make that first time out on the water a lot more fun and definitely a lot safer.

SELECTING A SITE

Seven tenths of the earth is covered with water, and a surprisingly large amount of that is suitable for boardsailing. But the beginner should be fairly discriminating when he selects the small piece of water where he will make his entry into the world of boardsailing. Ideally, you want a small body of water, such as a lake or a cove, where, no matter where you sail, drift, or get blown to, it won't be too far to paddle back to a shore. The other advantage of a small, relatively protected body of water

35

Beginners learn faster on calm waters and in light to moderate winds.

is that you are more likely to get the kind of wave-free conditions that are the most conducive to learning.

It is even more important to find a spot where there is a minimal amount of powerboat traffic. Not only is it disconcerting to have to dodge other boats when you haven't really learned to dodge yet, but also, no waves are as difficult to balance in, even for more experienced boardsailors, than the steep, irregular boat wakes that tend to come at you from every direction. At least, normal waves have a consistent pattern that you can get used to.

It would also be a good idea to find an area that is relatively current-free. Lakes and ponds are no problem, and there are also plenty of ocean sites where the tides have little effect. You just don't want to be in a position where you suddenly look up and find that, without your sailing an inch, a strong current has carried you far from your starting point.

And finally, you want an area where you get clear, undisturbed wind. Trying to learn to sail where tall trees, hills, or buildings interfere with the wind, causing it to swirl around and come from different directions at different strengths, is even more difficult and frustrating than trying to learn in waves or powerboat chop.

This isn't to say that the spot where you sail has to have all these characteristics or you won't learn. But the more of these requirements your learning spot can satisfy, the easier it will be for you. And while it is generally best to stay away from large, open bodies of water where the wind and seas are likely to be stronger and the danger exists of being blown or carried far from shore, even an exposed shoreline can serve as a safe learning site so long as you realize the potential drawbacks and dangers, don't try to sail when they are present, and are cautious when you do sail.

SELECTING CONDITIONS

The sea, or any body of water for that matter, should always be respected. Even at your ideal learning site, there are times when you are better off sitting on shore watching the more experienced boardsailors than out floundering around in conditions that are over your head. The best conditions for learning are light winds of approximately 4 to 8 knots. Anything much more and you are overpowered. And with anything much less, you just drift around without really sailing.

Get to know the different conditions where you're going to be sailing. In some areas, the prevailing winds may be consistently light or strong. In other areas, you may get light air one day and heavy the next. Or you may get thermal breezes, where the wind is light in the morning and gets stronger as the day progresses and the land temperature rises. Wind strength is often closely related to wind direction. In other words, the wind tends to be stronger from one direction and lighter from another, although which direction is light or strong generally varies in different areas.

The smaller and more protected a sailing site, the less the wind direction restricts suitable learning conditions. However, when learning on a fairly large, open body of water, it is extremely important to consider the wind direction before going out. An ideal wind direction for learning is one blowing parallel to the shore. The wind is usually steady, the seas aren't likely to be too large, and you can sail a course straight out and back with the wind at right angles each way, which is the easiest point of sail to master.

When the wind is blowing *onshore,* that is, toward shore, it is more difficult to get out to sail, both because you have to go against the wind and because there is a much greater likelihood of waves. But at least with an onshore wind, if you have any problems, you will always get blown back to shore. With an offshore wind (one blowing off the land out toward the body of water), a learner can have a lot of trouble getting back to shore. One of the big problems is that any offshore wind is deceiving. There are no waves close to shore, and the wind never feels as strong on land as it actually is out on the water. Also, wind coming over the land is very shifty and puffy, first blowing from one angle and then another, sometimes suddenly increasing in strength and sometimes decreasing. For all of these reasons, an inexperienced boardsailor should never attempt to sail on open water with the wind blowing offshore. You find yourself farther from shore with each fall that you take and faced with having to fight against the wind to get back in.

THE FAMILIARIZATION PROCESS

Before you actually get out and begin to learn how to boardsail, it's a good idea to familiarize yourself with your two basic components—the board and the sail —and the two basic elements they will be used in—water and wind. Getting used to the board on the water and the sail in the wind separately will make it that much easier to begin learning once you put the two together.

By finding and marking the balance points—the centerline and midpoint of a board —you can better follow the foot placement and weight distribution guidelines discussed throughout this book.

The Board

The best way to get a feel for how your board behaves on the water is to go out without the rig and just play around on it. But first you might find it helpful to locate and mark the balance points on your board with some tape or a magic marker. The *centerline* runs from the middle of the nose to the middle of the tail, through the maststep (where the mast is inserted) and the centerboard slot. The midpoint is found by picking up the board and locating where it balances between the nose and the tail. On most boards this will be somewhere between the front of the centerboard slot and the maststep. Where the centerline and the midpoint meet is the center of balance on your board. In other words, this is the point around which you will distribute your weight for the most effective balance on the water.

Once out on the water, paddle around, first with the centerboard in, and then out. Notice that the centerboard helps keep the board moving in a straight line and that the board turns by pivoting around the centerboard. This will be an important fact to remember later on when you begin steering with the sail. Next, stand on the board, first with your legs stiff and then with your knees

Paddling the Board

Paddling the board, both with and without the centerboard, gives you a feel for how it tracks and turns through the water.

Balancing Without the Rig

Learning to balance on the board without the rig prepares you for the actual sailing experience.

slightly bent. The second stance should feel far more comfortable and afford much better balance.

Standing with your feet just behind the midpoint line and straddling the centerline, rock the board from side to side, first gently and then more vigorously. Try it with your feet closer together, wider apart, standing in front of the midpoint line, standing farther back. See how far you can stand to one side of the centerline without losing your balance. See how far forward toward the nose and back toward the tail you can walk. Friends and I used to have contests to see who could get the farthest from the balance point without falling in. Not only do you get used to how your board feels, but you get used to the motion of the water, too. And while you're experimenting, keep in mind how much easier it will be to balance once you learn how to use the sail for support.

The Sail

In order to get some feel for the sail before you actually get out on the water, set your rig up in your board while it is sitting on the beach or on some other surface that won't damage the bottom, with the skeg removed. Hold the rig upright with your hand at the top of the uphaul line (with which you raise the rig) and let the sail rotate free. In this manner, the whole rig will act as a large weathervane. The back end of your booms will point in the direction that the wind is blowing.

You can get used to the feel of the sail and stay dry in the process by setting your board and rig up on the beach—just remove the skeg or dig a hole for it. This boardsailor practices trimming the sail, which, in this case, entails drawing it toward her with her back hand until the wind fills it.

A

B

C

D

Luffing

A sail luffs when the wind gets on either side of it. It luffs first in an area called "the luff" (shown in oval), right behind the mast *(A)*. The more you let the sail out (parallel to) the wind, the farther and farther back from the mast it luffs *(B,C)*, until the whole sail is luffing *(D)*.

Turn your board so that it is facing across the wind. This is the same relative position to the wind that you will want to start out with on the water. Thus, when you are standing on the board and letting the sail weathervane, holding the top of the uphaul line with your forward hand (the one closest to the board's nose), and your feet on either side of the maststep, the wind should be at your back, and you should be looking down the sail, which is approximately at right angles to the centerline of the board.

I call this the *ready position,* because it is the jumping-off point from which you actually begin to sail. This is a position you should become comfortable in and be able to hold as long as you can. From this position you will learn to turn the board to adjust your angle correctly to the wind. But most important, you will be able to pause in this position, think about what your next step is, and then do it when you are ready.

Keeping your knees bent and your body relaxed, just as you practiced on the water, experiment with moving the sail around. First, let the mast tilt away from you until the end of the booms almost touches the sand. Notice that you can lean back slightly with the rig helping you to balance. Now pull the mast slowly toward you. As it approaches a perpendicular position, you are less able to lean back. Pull it even closer to you, beyond perpendicular, and it is even more difficult to balance. Thus, the most stable position for the rig when you are in your ready position is with the mast leaning away from you with the end of the booms just clear of the water.

Now, still holding the uphaul with the forward hand and letting the sail weathervane, experiment with moving the rig forward and back, toward the nose and the tail. Notice that when the mast is perpendicular on the centerline, the sail flaps and shakes in the wind, gently if the wind is light, violently if the wind is strong. This is called *luffing,* and it occurs because the sail is in a neutral position, with the wind blowing equally on either side.

But when the mast is tilted to one side or the other, the back edge of the sail stops luffing. In other words, the back portion of the sail fills with wind on the side the mast is tilting toward. This would not be enough of the sail filled to make the board actually move forward through the water, but you should be able to feel a slight increase in pressure on that side, which will be important later when learning to turn the board.

With the board set up on the beach, you can also begin to try out and practice some of the on-the-water techniques discussed in later sections. Remember, this advance practice and familiarization under stable conditions on dry land will make it that much easier later on when you are having to deal with balancing the board on the water and the sail in the wind at the same time.

RIGGING TO SAIL

Every new sailboard comes with a set of rigging instructions that tell you how to put together the board, universal, mast, booms, and sail. These instructions are all relatively simple, with only minor variations from one brand to the next, and if you follow them closely, you shouldn't have any trouble getting rigged to sail. However, there are several important helpful rigging hints you should know that are generally not covered in the manufacturers' instructions.

Getting the Booms Tight

One of the greatest obstacles to learning to balance on a sailboard is loose booms. It's pretty difficult to gain any stability from the rig if the booms flops up and down against the mast every time you try to move them. Unfortunately,

The booms on this rig are too loose—they flop up and down against the mast. You can tighten them for better balance by retying the inhaul—the piece of line that holds them to the mast.

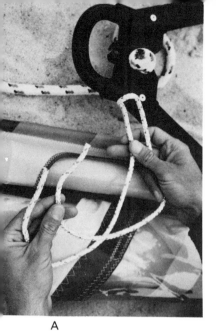

A

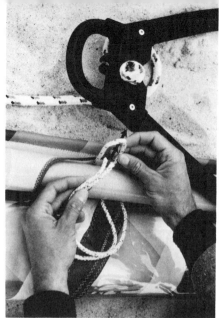

B

C

First, attach the inhaul to the mast *(A,B,C)*.

Getting the Booms Tight

Run both loose ends of the inhaul through any hole or holes in the boom handle *(E,F)*.

E

F

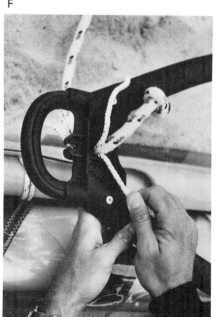

G

D

Next, with the mast and sail inside the booms, lay them parallel to each other *(D)*.

Now tie the two ends of the inhaul tightly around the mast so that the mast and boom end press together and there is no slack in the line *(G,H,I,J)*.

H   I   J

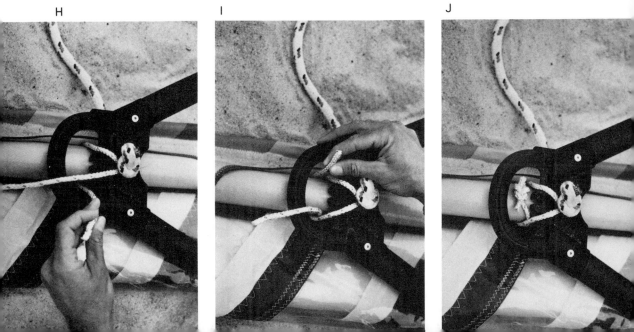

Getting the Booms Tight (Cont.)

K

L

Finally, lift the mast upright and slowly pull the boom down perpendicular to the mast *(K,L)*.

M

Your booms are now tight to the mast and ready to help you balance on the board and turn the rig while sailing *(M)*.

the methods most manufacturers recommend for attaching the booms to the mast seldom work. And because almost every manufacturer has a different kind of boom end, it is difficult to give specific instructions on a single method that will work in all cases. Therefore, you have to experiment and be a little creative in how you tie the inhaul, which is the line that attaches the booms to the mast.

One trick that will help, regardless of the type of boom end, is tying the mast to the booms while they are lying parallel, one on top of the other. Then, when the booms are pulled perpendicular to the mast and the outhaul attached and tightened, the inhaul and the mast/boom connection will tighten automatically. In fact, you sometimes have to be careful not to tie the inhaul too tight, because when the booms are brought perpendicular to the mast, they can tighten up so much that they actually crush or crack the mast's fiberglass. To help prevent this, wet the boom end where it will meet the mast so that there is less friction. Then pull the booms down slowly, being careful not to let them twist. If you hear anything starting to crack, or get extreme resistance, loosen the inhaul a little and try it again. In the end, you will be amazed at what a difference tight booms make to your balance.

Just a word on the height of the booms. Every sail has a cutout section in the sleeve where the booms are tied to the mast. Some sails even have two

An uphaul bungie keeps the uphaul within easy reach for raising the rig.

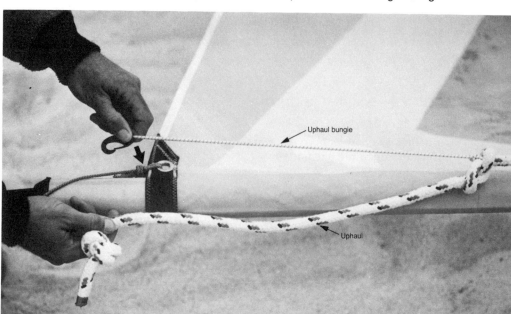

cutouts. This is so you can adjust the height of the booms to your own height or to the particular wind conditions. As a rule, while sailing, the learner should carry the booms about shoulder height. If they are too high, they can be awkward to handle, and if they are too much lower, you lose a lot of leverage. As you become more experienced, you can move the booms up above the shoulders, especially in heavy air, but most novices will find them easier to handle if they're not so high.

Optimizing the Uphaul

Another stock piece of equipment that needs some attention before you go out on the water is the uphaul, the line with which you pull the rig into an upright position. First, while you have your board and rig set up on the beach, stand on the board (with the skeg removed) with your feet on either side of the universal and with the sail lying in the sand. Tie a simple overhand knot in the end of the uphaul and begin to pull up the rig by the knot. Pull as far as you can with one hand, then reach out to get a new grip and continue to pull with the opposite hand. And each time you grab the uphaul, stop and tie another overhand knot just below your grip. In this way you will have three or four convenient nonslip grips, including the knot in the end, spaced on the uphaul exactly to your reach.

The second thing you want to do is make sure you have a good *uphaul bungie arrangement.* An uphaul bungie is a piece of shockcord that runs from the bottom of the uphaul to the top half of your universal. Thus the uphaul is always attached to a spot where you can reach it easily, without having to get down on your hands and knees to lean out over the water to retrieve it every time you have to pull the sail up. In many cases, an uphaul bungie is supplied with new boards. If not, you can easily rig one yourself. Just make sure that there is enough stretch in the piece of shockcord that it doesn't restrict the uphaul from pulling straight from the mast, otherwise you will be robbed of needed leverage. On the other hand, you don't want a piece so long that it flops around and gets underfoot when sailing. A good system is to tie the shockcord not to the bottom of the uphaul, but at the next knot up. This allows you to have a longer bungie for more range of pull, while at the same time keeping the uphaul taut and out of the way close to the mast.

There are two variations on the basic uphaul bungie system. One is to have a much longer piece of shockcord running from the uphaul down through an eye or loop at the top of the universal or in the downhaul and then leading up

A

When the outhaul of a rig is too loose, the sail bags against the booms and hinders a board's performance (A).

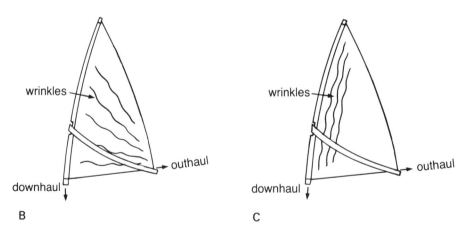

B   C

Diagram B shows the undesirable wrinkles in the sail when the outhaul is too tight, but the downhaul too loose.
   Diagram C shows the opposite—how the sail wrinkles when the outhaul is too loose, but the downhaul too tight.

to be tied off where the mast and booms meet. This provides you with maximum range of stretch while pulling on the uphaul and full retraction when not. The other system is a little tricky to make yourself, but it can be bought in most shops. This is a bungie uphaul with the shockcord inside a thick piece of woven, synthetic rope. The shockcord stretches until the rope reaches its length when lifting the sail, and then retracts to pull the uphaul back out of the way when not in use.

Achieving Proper Sail Shape

For the most part, sail shape adjustments are more the concern of the racer and advanced boardsailor, but there are some basic sail shape considerations that can make things easier for the learner. Your two basic adjustments are the outhaul, which determines how full or baggy the sail is, and the downhaul, which moves the fullness forward or back in the sail. A sail that does not have enough fullness will lack power to move the board, while a sail that is too full, or has its fullness too far forward or back, is difficult to control.

But you can't just come up with a single optimum sail shape, because you need different adjustments for different wind conditions. The best approach is to first adjust the outhaul so that the sail is about an inch away from touching the boom when the rig is held upright and the sail trimmed. The most common error among novices is to have the outhaul too loose, so that the sail drapes against the boom when filled with wind. If the outhaul is too tight, there is usually a long wrinkle or fold in the sail running parallel to the booms. The general rule is that you tighten the outhaul in heavy air and loosen it in light air.

Once the outhaul is properly adjusted, the downhaul is tightened or loosened so that there are no wrinkles or folds in the front of the sail near the mast. If the downhaul is too tight, there will be a vertical fold right next to the mast. And if the downhaul is too loose, there will be several horizontal wrinkles running back from the mast. As with the outhaul, you generally tighten the downhaul in strong winds and loosen it in light winds. In other words, you tighten it or loosen it along with the outhaul. Just remember to check your adjustments with the sail filled. Everything looks different depending on whether there is wind in the sail or not.

A

B

C

Rigging a Tether

Run a long piece of light line through the bottom of the centerboard slot (A), tie it around the bottom of the universal (B), put the centerboard in (C), and learn the beginning boardsailing techniques knowing your board is safely attached at the other end of the line to a buoy, an anchor, or a friend and won't drift far off (D).

D

Rigging a Tether

Next to the marginal sail, probably the single greatest aid to learning to board-sail is the tether. This simple homemade device is nothing more than 90 to 100 feet of light line tied at one end to your board, and at the other end to a mooring buoy, an anchor, or a dock, or even held by a friend. By being tethered to a stationary object, a beginner can avoid the most common and most frustrating problem encountered by learners—drifting far downwind and having to paddle back. Too, a tether allows you to sail on days when the wind direction might otherwise be unsafe for learning. A tether line gives you plenty of freedom to sail without having to worry about where you're going to end up.

This is an extremely important consideration. There's nothing more inhibiting to learning than to know that each fall is taking you farther from your starting point, that time spent climbing back on your board and pulling up the sail could mean just that much farther to paddle later on. A tether line frees you from worry and allows you to concentrate on the learning tasks at hand. If you get to the end of your rope (either literally or just figuratively), you can simply pull yourself back upwind and start fresh.

The best way to attach a tether to your board is to bring it up through the bottom of the centerboard slot and tie it to the centerboard handle or even the mast, so long as it doesn't get in the way of your feet. Never tie it directly to the nose or tail, since the line will then cause the board to turn upwind or downwind rather than pivot freely. Any strong, light line will work. Some people prefer line that floats, feeling that it causes less drag when sailing, but I prefer line that doesn't float, because there is then less chance of becoming ensnarled in it when turning.

LAUNCHING

Even for a relatively small person, carrying and launching a sailboard need not be difficult. As with boardsailing in general, it's not so much a matter of strength as planning and technique. For instance, the trick to carrying a rigged sail is to let the wind help you do the work. Holding the sail over your head with one hand on the boom and the other on the mast, keep the corner of the sail where the downhaul is located pointing into the wind. In this position, if you simply keep that corner tilted slightly up, the wind gets underneath and supports the rest of the sail while you carry it, sort of like a big kite. Just be careful not to lift the corner too high, especially in a strong wind, or the sail will try to take off on you. And don't dip the corner or let the wind get on top of the sail or it will try to dive on you. If there's not enough wind to help lift the sail, then you just carry it in the same way, resting it on your head.

As for carrying the board, there are two basic techniques. One is to carry it by your side with one hand in the centerboard slot and the other in the mast hole, which should balance the board nicely. The only problem with this technique is that can turn both you and the board while you're trying to carry it. In this case, the best technique is to carry the board over your head. It really doesn't take much strength. You just lift the tail, walk forward, place your head against the board a little behind the midpoint line, bend your knees, and lift with your hands on the rails forward of the line. It's kind of like doing an upside down headstand, and with the board flat, the wind doesn't turn it.

If you're launching off a sandy beach with nothing to damage your equipment, you can rig everything at the water's edge, attach the rig to the board, and then drag them out into the water. However, while you're dragging everything, it's a good idea to hold the rig by the mast or boom handle in one hand and the board by the nose or tail in the other, being careful to drag the board on its deck or rail rather than its bottom.

Another approach is to rig the sail and put it in the water first, since it won't float away while you go back to carry the board in. If you're launching off a dock, throw the sail as far out away from the dock as possible and then launch the board and paddle over to it. Even if you're launching off a beach,

Smart boardsailors let the wind help them carry the rigged sail to the water. Note the position of the boardsailor's hands on the mast and the booms.

Carrying the Board

To carry your board, simply stick a hand into the centerboard slot and balance the board under your arm with your other hand in the maststep.

To carry the board on your head, lift one end and walk forward under it until the board can pivot up on your head with only a little lifting.

When throwing your sail into the water preparatory to launching, throw on a flat plane so that the wind won't catch the sail and flip it.

When attaching the rig to the board, be sure to be in water deep enough to put the centerboard in without its scraping bottom. Note how this board-sailor has positioned the mast in line with the wind's direction, and the board and the booms perpendicular to it. This is the easiest position from which to lift the rig with the uphaul.

it's convenient to walk out a little and throw the sail into at least knee-deep water, where you can easily float the board out to the sail. If you attach the rig to the board in shallow water, you just have to drag them out to where it's deep enough to put the centerboard down.

One thing to remember is that all of these techniques are for launching in relatively calm water. They won't work if the waves get large enough to start breaking. When this happens to a novice, it's a good day not to go out. For the intermediates, the basic technique for lauching in waves is described on page 162.

LEARNING HOW TO FALL

Later on, I'll spend a complete chapter discussing boardsailing safety in general, but learning how to fall correctly and safely is a subject that needs to be covered right now. Falling into the water may be the easiest and most natural thing you encounter in boardsailing, and when you think about skiing, surfing, hang gliding, cycling, or any number of other sports, a fall in boardsailing is about as soft and safe as they come. It's not the landing that you need to concern yourself with. That will take care of itself. It's what you do before and after you hit the water that's important.

There are three things that novices sometimes feel nervous about when falling. One is landing on something, the second is having something land on them, and the third is ending up underneath the sail. For the novice, falling so that you land in the water and not against the board is mostly just a matter of resigning yourself to a fall when it's inevitable and bailing out rather than trying desperately to hold the rig up or to stay on the board. If you know you're going to fall, then do it and just make sure you fall away from the board and the rig.

When falling in backward, the big concern is that the rig will come over on top of you. The best way to prevent getting hit by the mast or booms in this situation is simply to keep holding onto the booms and thus keep them away from you when you hit the water. Or if you do let go, just keep a hand over your head when you go under and when you come back up again.

The other problem with the rig coming over on top of you is that you can sometimes find yourself under the sail. The main thing to remember here is that there is no need to panic. It's not a big sail, and you can easily get out from under it by moving forward or back along the boom. And the best way to do this is to just hold your breath and duck under water so that you won't be bumping against the booms or getting caught in the sail.

Falling

When falling, it is often wiser just to bail out rather than try to stay on the board and risk falling against it. Here the rig has overpowered the sailor, and he is getting pulled forward. By letting go of the rig and directing his fall away from the board, he avoids a potentially hard fall on the nose of the board or against the mast.

Falling Backward

When falling over backward, always hold onto the booms. That way, you avoid getting struck by the rig, and swimming out from under the sail is an easy matter.

Getting Caught Under Sail

This boardsailor has made the mistake of letting go of the rig as she falls in backward. Not only does she risk getting struck by the rig, she also faces a potentially harder time swimming out from under the sail.

4

Getting Started

You've been patient so far. You've found a good learning site, waited for the correct conditions, gotten used to the balance of the board on the water and the feel of the rig and sail on dry land, tightened your booms, rigged an uphaul bungie, adjusted your sail shape, and set up a tether. Now you're finally in the water and ready to start learning.

PULLING UP THE SAIL

You may think that there is nothing to pulling up the sail and the rig. Everyone knows how to pull, right? You just grab the uphaul and do it, right? Nothing could be further from the truth. The 180-pound strongman who tries to out-muscle the rig will have all sorts of trouble, while the 110-pound woman who develops the proper technique will have no trouble at all. Learning how to pull the sail up correctly is extremely important to the beginner mainly because he or she ends up having to do it so much. And two sure signs that you're not doing it correctly are early exhaustion and a nagging backache at the end of the day.

The best way to learn how to pull up the sail

61

As world-class boardsailor Nancy Johnson of Newport, Rhode Island, demonstrates, pulling up the sail needn't be difficult if you use the right techniques.

Pulling Up the Sail—
Board and Rig in the Most Common
Position to the Wind

A

B

With a bungie uphaul system there is no problem reaching the uphaul
to start pulling up the sail *(A,B)*.

C

D

Once you have hold of the uphaul, face straight down the mast, with your feet on the centerline and on either side of the universal (C).

Then lean back, making sure that your knees are bent and your shoulders are behind your knees so that you are pulling on the uphaul and the rig with your weight and legs rather than your back (D).

Pulling Up the Sail (Cont.)

E

F

The hardest part is just getting the sail free of the water—that is when you need to pull most. But as the sail begins slowly to come up, you'll find the sail feels progressively lighter, requiring less pull. Thus, you begin to straighten your legs and gradually lean back less. However, you still must be careful to keep your shoulders behind your knees and not pull with your back *(E)*.

At a certain point, usually when all the water has drained off the sail, the rig begins to come up relatively easily. To avoid pulling too hard and falling in backward, straighten up a bit more and begin pulling with your arms *(F)*.

G   H

The more the sail comes up, the more you straighten your body, pulling with your arms, and the less you lean back pulling with your weight until finally you are pulling the rig up the rest of the way entirely with your arms *(G,H,I,J)*.

Pulling Up the Sail (Conclusion)

I

J

is to start in shallow water, approximately waist deep (see page 56). Position the board so that it is pointing at right angles to the wind, just as you did on shore when familiarizing yourself with the sail. Then position the rig so that the mast is pointing in the same direction the wind is blowing and so the back of the sail is toward the back of the board. This is one of the easiest positions from which to pull up the sail. It is also one of the most common, since it is a position in which the sail is often likely to land when you fall.

Once on the board, grab the end of the uphaul line while kneeling and then stand and lean back so that the uphaul is supporting your weight. You can start out with either one or two hands on the uphaul, but I would recommend trying one hand for several reasons. First, this leaves the other arm free to help you balance. But more important, using one hand forces you to pull with your legs

This stance—unfortunately too common among novices—makes pulling up the sail more difficult than need be and usually leads to a sore back. Why? In straightening your legs and letting your shoulders get forward of your knees, your back is forced to do all the pulling, and at a point where the load is greatest.

Pulling Up the Sail—Variation 1:
Mast Downwind

A

B

When the mast is pointing in the same direction that the wind is blowing, but the end of the booms is toward the nose of the board (A), the board tends to turn in such a way that the nose points more into the wind as the sail is gradually pulled up (B).

C   D   E

This is not a problem if you move around the board so that you continue to look straight down the mast *(C,D,E)*. Moving this way ensures that your feet are always in a stable, centered position and that you are always pulling the mast straight up toward you.

Pulling Up the Sail—Variation 2: Mast Upwind

A

B

When the sail is in the water with the mast pointing into the wind, you can expect the board to turn a great deal when you start pulling the rig up. Again, this is no problem so long as you turn with the board, moving your feet around the universal so that you keep looking straight down the mast *(A,B,C,D,E)*.

D

E

As the board turns so that it is pointing in the opposite direction from where it started, the sail will fill with wind while the booms are still partially in the water, making it more difficult to lift any farther *(D)*.

The best technique in this situation is to hold what you've already pulled up until the board finishes its swing *(E)*.

C

F

At this point, the load on the sail dimin-
ishes—the wind begins to get under the
sail and actually helps to lift it—and you
can pull the rig up the rest of the way *(F)*.

G

When the booms break free of the water,
the sail flips around and you end up holding the rig in the ready position *(G)*.

A

B

Pulling Up the Sail—
Variation 3: Mast Upwind

Another technique for pulling the rig up when the mast is pointing toward the wind is to pull it around and over the nose or tail of the board so that it points in the same direction as the wind is blowing and is easier to pull up. Once again, the key to balancing is to move around the board so that you always face straight down the mast (A,B,C).

As you pull the sail around and over the board, don't try to pull it up until it is on the other side of the board (D,E), and then only hold what you've lifted until both the board and the sail stop turning.

Then, with the wind helping, pull the sail up. Note that when the booms break free of the water, the sail swings around and into a weathervaning position (F,G).

E

C

D

F

G

and weight. When you grab the uphaul with two hands, it tends to bend you over too far at the waist and cause you to pull with the back muscles.

Before you start pulling, position yourself so that you are looking straight down the mast with your feet on either side of the universal and as close to the centerline as possible. From this position you will be able to pull straight up toward you, which takes the least amount of effort and gives you the most balance. Your knees should be bent and you should be leaning back against the uphaul. The key to not pulling with your back is not to let your shoulders get too far forward of your hips and to use your legs. Make sure your uphaul is long enough, since one that is too short will automatically bend you forward at the waist.

Start pulling by leaning back and straightening your legs. Because of the weight of the rig and the water that is often in the sail, the mast will start coming up slowly, initially allowing you to lean back and really use your weight without being in any immediate danger of falling in backward. Don't try to jerk the sail up all at once. Even if you succeed, the sudden momentum when it breaks loose from the water will probably dump you in backward. Instead, pull slowly and steadily, allowing any water to drain off the back of the sail gradually.

At this point you should begin to feel less resistance. As the rig comes up it will become progressively lighter and progressively easier to pull. This is when you should begin using less body and legs and gradually pull more with your arms. If you don't, the sail will suddenly pop up and catch you leaning back too far. Essentially, what you are doing is taking the initial load of getting the sail free of the water with your weight and legs. But after that, you have better balance by shifting the pull to the arms. So you gradually go from pulling mostly with your body and a little with your arms, to equal body and arms, to a little body and mostly arms, to all arms. This shift in pull coincides with the need for progressively less leverage as the sail offers less resistance and for progressively more stability as the sail offers less aid to your balance.

Practice pulling the rig up from this position until you feel comfortable with the technique. Next, with the board in the same relative position to the wind, practice pulling the rig from the water in different positions relative to the board: (1) with the rig downwind and the back of the sail toward the nose of the board; (2) with the rig upwind and the back of the sail toward the nose; (3) with the rig upwind and the sail toward the tail.

From these positions, you stand the same way and pull the same way, but there are some variations. For instance, as you pull the mast up with the rig in these positions, the sail is more likely to fill with wind before it is completely

A   B

Picture *A* is a good example of what happens when your feet aren't on the centerline and you don't move around the board to stay in line with the mast (looking straight down it) when it turns as you pull the sail up. Your weight ends up too much on one side of the board and your body lean is not balanced against the weight of the rig. The result? A backward fall *(B)*. Note that instead of falling *away* from the board when the fall became inevitable, this sailor tried to stay on the board and has fallen against the sail.

out of the water, thus causing the board to turn. Don't be concerned. Just hold what you have already pulled up and let the board turn, while at the same time moving around the mast base so that you can keep looking straight down the mast. Eventually the board will turn to a position where it will stop, and the wind will actually help you lift the sail the rest of the way. As you become more experienced, you will be able to continue to lift the sail even while the board is turning, but initially it is better just to concentrate on balancing until the board stops moving.

Pulling the sail up when it's lying upwind adds another dimension—it's on the opposite side of where it's going to end up once the wind fills it. A quick, agile, experienced boardsailor can simply lift the sail, let the wind get under it, and let it swing around to the downwind side. But this is a pretty tricky maneuver for the novice to pull off without losing his balance and going for a swim. Instead, the rig should be pulled around over the nose or the tail, depending on which end of the board the mast is closer to, into a position where the sail is downwind of the board. Just remember that no matter where the board and rig start out, you won't have any trouble learning how to pull up the sail as long as you are patient, let the board turn when and where it wants to, bend at the knees, gradually transfer the pull from the body to the arms, and never pull with the back.

The Ready Position

A

The ready position. The most stable ready position is with the rig and sail leaning slightly away from you so that the end of the booms is just out of the water and you can lean back slightly against the pull of the rig *(A)*.

B

Incorrect ready position. The mast is much more difficult to balance when pulled up to the perpendicular *(B)*. Note in both pictures, though, the sailor's feet are over the centerline and on either side of the midline, and his knees are bent. This puts the sailor's weight in the most stable position and his body in the most relaxed position for balancing.

TURNING IN PLACE

Before you can trim the sail and actually start sailing, it is important for the board to be in a position with the wind at your back blowing at right angles to the centerline. This position relative to the wind, called *reaching*, is the easiest position from which to first trim the sail. If the wind is coming either more from the nose or the tail, getting started is much more difficult.

The problem, as we already know, is that the board often turns while the rig is being lifted. There is no guarantee that the board will be in a reaching position once you pull the sail up, even if everything was set up in the correct position while the rig was still in the water. Thus, you need to learn how to turn the board in place and position it to the wind. This is what I like to call a *stationary turn*, because it is done in one spot without actually sailing. It is also commonly called a *rope turn*, because it is performed holding onto the uphaul.

Once you've pulled the rig up, regardless of which direction the board is facing, you should get in the same ready position that you learned on shore when familiarizing yourself with the sail and rig. In other words, you should be standing with your back to the wind, facing down the weathervaning sail, holding the rig up with one hand at the top of the uphaul, your knees bent slightly, and your shoulders approximately over the hips. The mast should be leaning away from you at an angle that just allows the end of the booms to stay clear of the water. If the end of the booms does touch the water for any length of time, the sail will not be able to turn freely in the wind. In effect, the sail will trim itself and cause you to start sailing or turning out of control. On the other hand, if the mast is held too upright, the rig becomes a hindrance to your balance rather than a help.

From the correct ready position described above, you can do a stationary turn in either direction simply by tilting the mast to one side or the other. Let's say, for example, that in pulling up the sail, the board has swung around and is facing into the wind, which is a relatively common occurrence. To get the board turned back into a position where the wind is at right angles to the centerline, you just lean the sail in the opposite direction from the way you want to turn. Keep the mast tilted, moving around its base as the board turns, until the nose is pointing in the direction you want to start sailing. Then you just straighten the mast up to stop turning.

Turning the Board

A

K

WIND

B

To turn the board in order to position it to the wind, extend your arm and the mast in the direction you want to turn *(A,B)*. Of course, as the board turns, you must move around the base of the mast so that you continue to look down the booms *(C–K)*. In essence, the sail and rig remain in the same position relative to the wind, while the board turns

C

D

WIND

WIND

J

I

beneath both you and the sail. To continue turning, keep your arm and the mast extended to your side. To stop, bring your arm and mast back in front of you, as in the ready position. This technique enables you to turn the board 360 degrees in either direction.

H

E

F

G

What you are doing is using the weathervane effect of the sail to turn the board. In other words, the sail is held stationary by the wind, and you turn the board around it. By tilting the mast to one side, you allow gravity to trim the sail slightly, filling just the back portion of it, which in turn acts as a lever to push the nose or the tail of the board in the opposite direction, pivoting it around the centerboard. Practice this until you can do complete circles in either direction. Then you will be able to get into your reaching position to start sailing, no matter what direction you're facing after the sail is pulled up.

TRIMMING AND GETTING STARTED

With the board in the reaching position and you in your ready position, you should be holding the uphaul in your forward hand. Remember, this is a position where you can pause and think about what you're doing and what comes next. What comes next are the steps you go through to trim the sail— that is, draw it toward you and into the wind—and to start sailing. The first step, once you're ready to proceed, is to grab the mast with your back hand and then reach across with your forward hand and grab the boom approximately a foot back from the mast. Now you can let go of the mast and hold the rig up by the boom with your forward hand reaching across your body.

As demonstrated by Platt Johnson, Newport, Rhode Island, start in the ready position *(A)*. Cross your front hand over your back hand and grab the boom about a foot back from the mast *(B)*. Let go of the mast with your back hand and pull the mast

A   B

Trimming the Sail

Remember to keep your knees slightly bent and your feet on either side of the universal near the centerline. (Actually, your front foot is just forward of the mast, and your back foot is about a foot behind it.) Also, don't let your body bend forward at the waist or let the end of the booms drag in the water.

In this position, the sail and rig should still be able to rotate freely in the wind. Do not try to trim it yet or restrict it in any way. As with your ready position, this is a position that you should be able to hold. This is your last chance to stop for a moment and consider just what it is that you have to do. Don't go on to the next step until you're sure you're ready. Once you've begun, there is no further opportunity to hesitate or be tentative. When you are ready, pull the mast up to and just forward of your forward shoulder. Then immediately grab the boom with your free hand about shoulder width back from your front hand and trim in.

The mechanics of these three final steps—cross forward hand over and grab boom, pull mast to shoulder, and trim—are carefully designed to avoid some common mistakes that the beginning boardsailor invariably makes when first starting to sail. For example, if you grab the boom first with your back hand, instead of crossing over with your forward hand, it is difficult to hold the sail so that it continues to rotate freely. The back hand tends to trim the sail before you're ready for that step.

up to and forward of your front shoulder *(C)*. Grab the boom slightly more than shoulder width back from your front hand *(D)*. Pull the boom toward your body with your back hand to trim the sail and start sailing *(E)*.

C

D

E

Improper Trimming Technique

A

B

If you don't pull the mast all the way up to and forward of your front shoulder *(A)*, you are forced to bend forward at the waist *(B)*, when you grab the boom with your back hand, and when you trim the sail two things happen: (1) you are forced to use your back muscles to keep from getting pulled overboard by the sail *(C)*, since it has leverage on you; and (2) the board turns up into the wind *(D)*, because the sail is too far back toward the tail, often resulting in the board turning into the wind, the whole sail luffing, and you falling in backward.

C

D

And if you don't pull the mast up to your shoulder for the second step, when you reach for the boom with your back hand to trim it, you will be forced to bend forward at the waist, which immediately puts you off balance, increasing your chances of being pulled in by the sail and putting you in a position where you are using your back muscles. In addition, if you don't pull the mast up *forward* of your shoulder, the sail will be too far back toward the tail when trimmed and will cause the board to turn toward the wind rather than sail straight ahead. This in turn results in the sail luffing, the wind being spilled, and, usually, the sailor falling in backward.

These are the two most common types of falls for the beginning boardsailor: getting pulled in frontward by the sail, and pulling the sail over and falling in backward. The best way to avoid them is simply to bring the mast up to the correct position before trimming in the first place.

But if you find that you have erred in this step and are being pulled over by the sail, you can still save yourself a fall by quickly letting go of the boom with your back hand, at which point the sail harmlessly luffs and you can straighten up and try it again the correct way—without bending forward at the waist. Don't, under any circumstances, let go of the boom with your forward hand. The back hand will keep the sail trimmed, the unsupported front of the rig will spin around, and at the very least you will drop the sail, if you don't end up in the water as well.

To save a fall backward, if you haven't brought the mast far enough forward before trimming and find yourself turning up into the wind, again let

A

B

Recovery from improper trimming technique. If you find that you are bending forward at the waist and the sail is beginning to pull you over *(A),* you can recover your balance and leverage simply by letting go of the boom with your back hand *(B).* This allows the sail to weathervane, eliminating its pull. After that, you can start to trim all over again, this time being sure to pull the mast up to you rather than leaning over to grab the boom.

If the sail is pulling you over *(A)*, don't try to recover by letting go of the boom with the forward hand *(B)*. If you do, the front of the sail, instead of weathervaning, will twist away and pull you into the water *(C)*.

A

go with your back hand, then quickly step around to the front of the mast, grab the uphaul, and do a stationary turn to get back into a reaching position where you can take another try at trimming correctly.

As for the final trimming step, it is important to pull the boom straight in toward your back shoulder with your back hand. This avoids a tendency to pull the whole sail back toward the tail when trimming, which, as we know, rounds the board up into the wind. It is also important to trim in far enough so that the sail stops luffing completely. If it is trimmed in only partially, the front of the sail will continue to luff while the back of the sail is filled. This imbalance is another common cause of the board rounding up into the wind.

Just a word about foot placement. The reason you have your back foot farther behind the mast when trimming than when pulling up the sail is that, first, you give yourself a wider stance for better balance, and second, you give yourself some leverage to push with your front foot to help keep the board from rounding up.

One final note—you can practice all the trimming steps on shore. If you can get the correct positioning down and get so you can go through the steps smoothly and even almost automatically with your board and rig set up on the beach, you'll be sailing that much quicker when you get out on the water.

B

C

Paddling the Board

If the wind and waves aren't too strong, it's an easy matter to position the rig with the booms resting on the tail of the board, then lay yourself stomach-down on the board and paddle with your arms fully extended.

A

B

E

F

Furling the Sail

In rough conditions, it's best to furl the sail. Start by uncleating the outhaul *(A)* and separating it from the sail *(B)*. Then remove the universal from its slot *(C)*, set the mast across the board and roll the sail against the mast *(D,E)*. With the booms parallel to the mast, secure the sail by tying the outhaul and the uphaul around the sail and mast *(F,G,H,I)*. Then set the rig on the board and paddle *(J)*.

C

D

G

H

I

J

5

Sailing

You're sailing. Once you've managed to trim the sail and start moving forward without falling in the water or rounding up into the wind, you are honestly sailing. If you've never sailed before in your life, it's a thrill you won't forget. Even if you've sailed before, the first time you get going on a sailboard you'll feel the excitement all over again. You are actually moving across the water on a sailboard that is powered by the wind and directly controlled by your body. You're on the threshold of a whole new world of experience. Now all you have to do to strike out into that new world is gain more control by learning to steer, adjust sail trim, and sail at different angles to the wind.

STEERING

You've already had some experience with the techniques and mechanics of steering a sailboard. For instance, you've already seen that a board can be turned in a stationary position by tilting the sail to one side or the other. And you also know from experience that unless the mast is brought up in front of the forward shoulder when trimming, the board will turn into the wind.

89

Blue skies and a gentle breeze are the perfect complements to a day on the water.

Steering

Once you are sailing, you steer by tilting the rig toward the nose or tail of the board.

As the center of the sail is brought back toward the centerboard, the board turns more gradually *(F)*.

Steering—turning downwind. When the rig is tilted toward the nose, the center of the sail and more of the force of the wind are forward of the pivot point at the centerboard. Thus, the tail turns toward the wind, the nose turns away from the wind, and the board turns *downwind (D,E).*

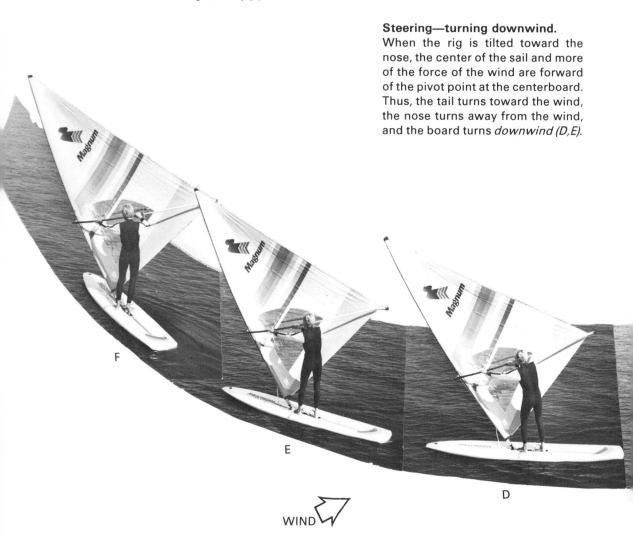

F

E

D

WIND

Steering—turning upwind. When the rig is tilted toward the tail, the center of the sail—and thus more of the force of wind—is behind the centerboard, causing the tail to pivot away from the wind and the nose to pivot toward the wind *(B,C)*. As a result, the board turns so that it is sailing more upwind.

When the center of the sail is directly over the centerboard, you sail in a straight line *(A)*.

C

B

A

To steer a sailboard while sailing, you simply *tilt the rig toward the nose to head down away from the direction the wind is blowing and tilt the rig back toward the tail to head up toward the wind.* How far you tilt the sail in either direction and how long you leave it tilted determines how fast and how far you turn. And when you finish turning or adjusting your course, you simply bring the rig back to a balanced position, which is generally with the mast tilted slightly toward the nose, so that the board again steers a straight course.

The basic theory behind turning or steering a sailboard is based on changing the position of the center of the sail relative to the position of the centerboard. In a balanced position, with the center of the sail directly over the centerboard, the board should sail in a straight line. But when the sail is tilted toward the nose, it puts more sail area forward of the centerboard and pushes the nose away, steering you downwind. And when you tilt the sail toward the tail, more of the sail is in back of the centerboard, pushing the tail away and steering the nose up toward the wind. In essence, the board is steered by being pivoted around the centerboard by the sail.

When first sailing, you should simply try to steer as straight as possible. Even before trimming, pick out an object such as a buoy or something on shore that you are already heading toward when you're in your ready position with the board at right angles to the wind. The trick is to keep your board as close as possible to this same angle to the wind by steering directly for the target you have selected. Being able to steer a straight course is important for two reasons. The most obvious one is that the shortest distance between two points is a straight line. More important is that each time the direction you're steering changes, you have to adjust your sail trim to compensate for the wind coming from a different angle, not to mention that you have to tilt the sail forward or back to get headed in the direction you want to go again. But the most important reason is that wandering too far off course can often leave you in a position where it is difficult to get either where you want to go or back to your starting point.

Sailing upwind and downwind is like climbing up and down a hill. It's easy to go down, but it takes a little work to get back up again. Reaching—sailing at right angles back and forth across the wind—is like going across the hill. It's neither easier nor harder. But if you let yourself steer too much down away from the wind, which is often a natural tendency for the learner, you have to head "uphill" against the wind to get back. If you have a tether, there is no real problem, since all you have to do is reel yourself back in. But if you have advanced beyond the tether, then you can find yourself wandering off downwind, or "downhill," unable to get back to the beach or the dock without paddling. Thus it is a good idea to get so you can consistently steer a straight course across the wind before abandoning the tether.

When trying to steer a straight line, avoid oversteering. This is a common problem caused by trying to correct a course variation too quickly and too radically. A familiar scenario when finding yourself a little below your course is to tilt the sail too far back to correct and end up steering way above your course. You should be able to make minor adjustments by tilting the rig just slightly forward or back. Sometimes it helps to think of the straight line you're steering as being a wide line or lane that allows some minor course variations that don't really take you away from whatever you're steering for. Another aid is to look back every once in a while at your wake through the water. If it is not straight, it should at least be curving gradually within a narrow range. If it is radically irregular, it indicates that you are oversteering.

One final helpful hint is to steer slightly above, or upwind, of your target. If you are going to err in your course, it is better to end up slightly to the upwind side. You can always sail back down easily, which is not the case if you err to the downwind side. Also, since the wind is constantly trying to push the board downwind, there is always a little sideslipping, even while moving forward. So it is good to compensate for this by heading a little more upwind than you think you have to—just to make sure.

ADJUSTING THE SAIL

When adjusting the position of the sail by pulling it in or letting it out, there is an exact point where the sail will provide maximum speed and efficiency for the given wind direction and strength. This is the position where the sail is neither too far out nor too far in; in other words, neither undertrimmed nor overtrimmed. When the sail is undertrimmed, it luffs, spills wind, and causes you to sail slower. The more the sail is eased out, sometimes called "sheeted out," the more it luffs and the slower you sail, until it is let out all the way and you come to a stop. When you trim it in again, you start moving again.

Thus the back arm acts like an accelerator, controlling your speed through the position of the sail and the amount of luff. If you want to slow down because you are uncomfortable with your speed or are having trouble with control or for any other reason, you simply ease the sail out until you have slowed down to the desired speed. One important point to remember here is that when the sail is allowed to luff partially, it tends to try to turn the board up into the wind, as we have already discussed. Therefore, as you begin to let the sail luff to slow down, you need also to keep the whole rig forward and push with your front foot to keep the board from rounding up.

As for accelerating, there is a common misconception that if you speed up when you trim the sail a little, and go a little faster when you trim the sail a little more, then the farther you trim, the faster you will go. This is true only up to the point where the whole sail just stops luffing. If it is trimmed beyond this point, not only do you not continue to accelerate, but instead you begin to sail slower. This is called overtrimming and means that you are restricting the movement of the wind over the sail and thus limiting the sail's ability to turn all the power of the wind into forward motion.

When you start out sailing on a reach, with the wind at right angles to the board, the correct trim position will be with the sail about halfway between all the way out and all the way in. But this tells you only roughly where to trim the sail. To find the exact position for the most efficient sail trim on a reach, watch the spot just behind the mast where the sail stops luffing last when trimmed and starts luffing first when eased. Trim in just to the point where this spot stops luffing and then trim no farther. If you're not certain whether you are overtrimmed or not, try letting the sail out just a little. If it luffs, then the sail was in the correct position and you just trim back in to it. But if it doesn't luff, that means you are overtrimmed and have to keep letting the sail out slowly until it just luffs. Then pull it in to the point where it just stops luffing.

Never assume that once you find the most efficient sail trim position that it will stay that way. As your course varies slightly and the wind intermittently changes direction, the position of optimum sail trim changes as well. A good sailor learns to keep checking the sail, adjusting it to keep it trimmed to the correct position and working at its maximum.

TURNING AROUND

Even while you're mastering steering and adjusting sail trim, you need to be able to turn around so that you can sail back and forth across the wind at right angles. You need to be able to sail away from the beach or the dock on a reach and then turn around and sail back again on a reach. To accomplish this, you use a *rope turn,* which is basically the same as the stationary turn you use to position yourself and your board to the wind before trimming.

To begin a rope turn while sailing on a reach, first let go of the boom with your back hand. Then, with the back hand, you reach across your forward arm, which is still holding the weathervaning rig by the boom, and grab the uphaul

Good reaching sail trim. When the wind is from the side of the board, you are *reaching,* and the sail should be approximately halfway out. In this way you get maximum work from the sail, which is as far out as it will go without luffing.

Undertrimmed. If the back hand lets the sail out too far— in this case beyond the halfway point—the sail luffs along the mast and the board slows down. The farther beyond the perfect trim position the sail is let out, the more it luffs and the slower the board sails. In this position, the sail is described as *undertrimmed.*

Overtrimmed. To pull a sail *in* beyond the point where it stops luffing is called *overtrimming,* and the board not only slows down, but also begins to slip sideways.

The Rope Tack

WIND

B

C

D

A

To do a rope tack, release the booms, grab the uphaul, and tilt the mast and sail toward the tail of the board (A).

As the board turns toward the wind, move around the front of the mast, still tilting the sail in the same direction. In this sequence, as the sail is moved to the right, the board turns facing the wind (B,C).

As the board continues to turn, you move around to the opposite side (D).

E

Once the board is pointing in the new direction you want to sail (E), use the crossover grip, pull the mast up toward your forward shoulder, grab the boom with your back hand, trim the sail in, and go.

The Rope Jibe

E

Once the board has turned all the way around and is facing in the direction you want to sail, and you are standing on the opposite side of the board *(D,E),* use your crossover grip, pull the mast up to your forward shoulder, trim the sail in with your back hand, and start sailing again.

You generally do a rope jibe instead of a rope tack when you are already heading more away from the wind than toward it, since it is then the shorter distance to turn. It begins like a rope tack in that you release the booms and grab the uphaul *(A).*

D

As the board turns, you move around the universal base, continuing to tilt the mast in the same direction to your side *(C)*.

C

However, instead of tilting the mast toward the tail as in a rope tack, you tilt the mast *toward the nose* which turns the board away from the wind *(B)*.

B

A

WIND

close to the top. Now, if you let go of the boom with your forward hand, you are essentially in your ready position, except that you are probably still moving forward some on your momentum.

From this position, you have a choice between two different kinds of rope turns, a rope tack or a rope jibe, depending on whether you want to turn around into the wind or away from the wind. A *rope tack,* which is the most commonly used of the two, is when you turn into the wind. As soon as you are holding the rig by the uphaul, you tilt the mast back toward the tail, and the board responds by turning toward the wind. As you keep the mast tilted in the same position, the board turns under it, and you move around the mast in the opposite direction it is turning.

Even when the board has turned so that it is facing directly into the wind, you keep the mast tilted in the same direction, which is now to the side opposite from the direction the board is turning. At this point you move to the nose of the board and then, as you continue to turn, to the opposite side from which you started. Finally, the board comes to a reaching position facing back in the direction you just sailed from. Now you straighten up the mast to stop turning and find yourself in your ready position, set to reach across your back hand, grab the boom, pull the mast up forward of your shoulder, trim, and begin sailing again.

To do a *rope jibe,* the process is basically the same. The only difference is that you tilt the mast toward the nose and turn away from the wind, moving around the back of the board as it turns, instead of around the front. But you still keep the mast tilted until you are on the opposite side of the board and headed in the opposite direction on a reach. And you still end up in a ready position, set to go through the same steps of trimming to get sailing again.

Whether you choose to do a rope tack or a rope jibe usually depends on which turn requires the shorter distance. In other words, if you are already heading more toward the wind than a reaching course, it is generally more convenient and faster to tack. And if you are heading more away from the wind than a reaching course, then you are already closer to jibing. But when you are reaching and therefore an equal distance from tacking or jibing, tacking is the easier maneuver. Also, in stronger winds or seas, tacking is more stable than jibing. But in the beginning, it is important to learn and to practice both tacking and jibing, so that you can turn in whichever direction safety or convenience dictates.

So far you have learned to do all of your sailing back and forth on a reach, pretty much in a straight line, and all of your turning with rope turns. But there are other positions of sailing and other types of tacks and jibes. And with them comes a whole new dimension of boardsailing freedom and mobility.

Points of Sail

As you already know, reaching is when you are sailing at right angles to the wind. It is only one of several different *points of sail* that allow you to sail any number of angles or directions relative to the wind. When you sail at less than right angles to the wind—in other words, more *toward* the wind or upwind— you are said to be sailing more *closehauled*. And when you sail at more than right angles to the wind, more *away* from the wind or downwind, you are said to be sailing more *offwind*.

Points of Sail

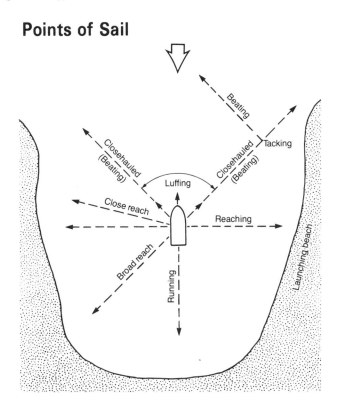

There are degrees of upwind and downwind sailing. When you sail as far offwind as you can, with the wind coming directly over the tail, you are *running* before the wind. And if you are sailing at more than a right angle to the wind, but not directly before it, you are *broad reaching,* which is basically a course halfway between reaching and running, relative to the wind. When you are on a broad reach, the wind is coming at an angle from the side and from behind, roughly over the corner of the tail.

Sailing upwind is a little different, namely because you can't sail directly toward the wind the way you can sail directly away from it. You've already seen that when the wind blows equally on both sides of the sail, it luffs and you can't get the board moving until the sail is trimmed. But it is impossible to trim the sail so that the board will move straight into the wind. In fact, the closest you can sail toward the wind effectively is about 45 degrees. This is called *beating.* And when you are sailing at an angle somewhere in between beating and reaching, it is called *close reaching,* because you are sailing a little closer into the wind than when on a reach.

It is not absolutely necessary to know all the names of the different points of sail by heart, but it is important that you be able to sail them. When you start out to expand your horizons from just reaching back and forth across the wind, do it gradually and systematically. First pick a spot to steer for that is just a little upwind of where the board is pointing when you are in a reaching position. When you trim and start sailing, it should still be from the reaching position, but once you get going, you steer up for a new target.

To do this, of course, you will tilt the rig toward the tail and then straighten it back up once you are headed in the direction you want to go. From this point it is just the same as steering on a reach. You try to steer as straight a course as possible, aiming a little upwind of your target to account for the board sideslipping. The only difference is that you will have to trim the sail in a little more to keep it from luffing.

Then when you turn around—probably tack—to sail back to your starting point, you will be sailing more offwind, and you will be able to let the sail out a little farther without it luffing. Don't forget that if the sail isn't as far out as it can go without luffing, it is overtrimmed and you are not sailing as fast or as efficiently as you could.

Practice sailing back and forth at these angles until you feel comfortable and confident with the steering and trimming. Then pick an object even farther upwind. This will mean trimming the sail in still farther when going more upwind in one direction and letting it out more when sailing more downwind going back the other way. Using this process, you will gradually be able to sail new angles progressively more upwind and downwind. Just remember that, although you know roughly where the sail should be trimmed according to your angle to the wind, to fine trim it to the exact correct position, you have to watch the front of the sail and adjust to the luff.

Beating and Tacking

To begin beating, pick an object to steer for that will give you a course of about 45 degrees to the wind. To steer this course, you have to trim the sail approximately off the corner of the tail. Except when beating in strong winds, this is as far as you should ever trim the sail. To bring the sail in any farther would be overtrimming and would cause you to lose speed and would increase sideslipping. If you have your sail trimmed to this position and it still luffs, it means that you are trying to sail closer to the wind than is possible. When this is the case, you have to steer for a different object, one just slightly downwind from your original upwind target.

But what if the beach or dock you want to get back to is too far upwind

Running. When the wind is directly from behind, the position of sailing is called *running.* Note that the sail is in proper position when it is all the way out and square to the wind, and that the sailor is standing behind the mast instead of next to it.

Beating. In the beating position, the sail is trimmed approximately to the corner of the tail and you sail as close into the wind as you can without the sail luffing. When beating, you are sailing *upwind,* which is also called *sailing closehauled.*

Overtrimming when beating. When you are beating, your sail should be pulled to about the corner of the tail (see illustration, page 103). If you try to pull the sail in much beyond this point, you are overtrimmed, and not only do you sail slower, but the board also slips sideways.

Undertrimming when beating. Here, the wind is from 45 degrees in front of the board, but the sailor has trimmed the sail only halfway, as if the wind were from the side. As a result of this undertrimming, the sail luffs; the board loses speed until the sail is trimmed in to the corner to stop it from luffing.

Pinching. If you try to sail closer to the wind (by overtrimming beyond the corner of the tail) in order to steer up more without the sail luffing, you may succeed in pointing the nose of the board more *toward* the wind, but the board will sideslip, and you will actually sail a course more *away* from the wind.

to steer for without having to luff or overtrim? Or what do you do if you have to get to a spot that is directly upwind? You already know that you can't steer directly where you want to go in these instances. Instead, you get there by sailing a zigzag course, much in the same way someone might plan a route to climb a mountain that is too steep to go straight up. In other words, you sail as close to the wind as you can in one direction, and then tack and sail as close to the wind as you can in the other direction. In this manner you eventually work your way upwind to where you want to go.

At this point, because of the importance of tacking when beating upwind, it is time to learn a more advanced type of tack than the rope tack. Actually, the advanced tack uses the same basic principle of the rope tack. You still use the sail to turn by tilting the rig back, and you gradually move around the front of the board to the opposite side as it returns. But with an advanced tack you don't let go of the boom and make your turn while holding onto the uphaul. Nor do you let the sail luff throughout the turn.

Instead, when you begin an advanced tack, you keep the sail trimmed with your back hand as you tilt the mast toward the tail. As the board turns toward the wind you gradually trim the sail farther, in essence overtrimming slightly, so that it doesn't luff even though you are heading closer than 45 degrees into the wind. And as the board continues to turn, you move forward, quickly letting go of the boom and grabbing the mast with your forward hand. By the time the nose is straight into the wind, you should be standing in front of the mast with your back to the wind, one hand still on the mast and the other still on the boom.

Continue trimming with your back hand so that the sail is pulled around slightly and still filled. This is called *backing* the sail. It serves to turn the nose out of the wind on the opposite side. Then you can let go of the boom and grab the opposite boom. Thus your back hand before and during the tack becomes the forward hand after the tack. You now let go of the mast, grab the boom with your new back hand, trim in, and begin sailing on a beat in the new direction. One thing to remember when tacking to a beat is that you are trimming on a closehauled course rather than on the reaching course that you have been following up until now. This means that you have to make sure that the mast and rig are tilted far enough forward when you trim that the board doesn't round back up into the wind. This is a common problem when advancing beyond a rope tack. Something else that will help to avoid this problem is to consciously push with your forward foot to keep the nose from coming up into the wind.

The Advanced Tack

With an advanced tack, the board turns in the same direction as with a rope tack—toward the wind. This time, though, keep the sail trimmed as you tilt the rig back instead of releasing your hold of the booms and letting the sail luff *(A,B).*

Even when the nose is pointing directly into the wind, continue trimming the sail with your back hand to keep the board turning as you move around in front of the mast *(C).*

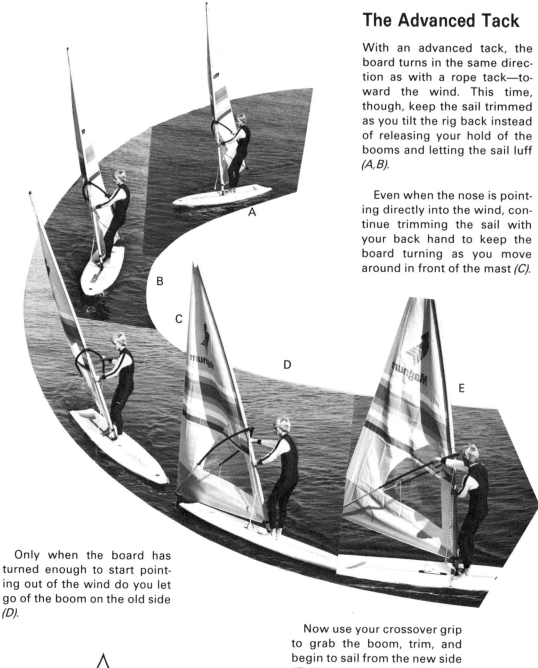

A

B

C

D

E

WIND

Only when the board has turned enough to start pointing out of the wind do you let go of the boom on the old side *(D).*

Now use your crossover grip to grab the boom, trim, and begin to sail from the new side *(E).* Notice that when tilting the rig back and moving around the mast, the forward hand is moved to the mast while the back hand continues to pull in the boom.

While running is an easy point of sail for the beginner, since you are simply being pushed in the same direction the wind is blowing, it does require a slightly different technique from reaching and beating. First of all, keep in mind that if you sail directly downwind from your starting point, you will eventually have to beat and tack upwind to get back. This is no problem once you have mastered the necessary upwind skills, but if you are not yet accomplished at beating, you should be careful not to get too far downwind. It doesn't take very long to get down there, but it can take quite a while to get back up again. It might even be best to beat and tack upwind and then practice running downwind rather than the other way around.

Another big difference in running is that you stand directly behind the mast, facing forward, and steer by tilting the sail from side to side instead of facing sideways and tilting the sail front and back. Also, because of your position on the board and the position of the sail, running can be potentially more unstable. When beating or reaching, the sail offers an aid to your balance across the board, which is the narrowest and least stable plane. But when running, you don't have this aid and must therefore rely on your own balance to steady the board from side to side.

The best position for achieving good balance when running is standing about a foot and a half behind the midline with your feet about halfway in from the rails. Your knees should be slightly bent and your back relatively straight, much the same as the stance used for reaching and beating. A conscious effort should be made to keep the weight evenly balanced over both feet. However, don't make the mistake of overbalancing, which is somewhat similar to over-steering. The board can roll fairly far without dumping you in the water, so you don't have to try to keep it perfectly level. You're better off relaxing and keeping the rolling under control with minor weight adjustments rather than overdoing the side-to-side balancing.

The other balance dimension you have to be aware of is the potential for getting pulled over forward by the rig. Just as when reaching or beating, you prevent this by keeping the knees bent, by not leaning forward at the waist, and by not letting the rig lean downwind, in this case toward the nose.

As for steering, you tilt the rig to the side opposite from the direction you want to turn. The principle is the same. You're putting more sail area to one side of the centerboard, which forces the board to turn the opposite direction by pivoting around the centerboard. Be careful not to lean toward the side you are tilting the rig. Instead, simply extend your arms to the side, keeping the rest

F

E

G

Steering Downwind

When steering while running before the wind (A), the technique is different from tacking or jibing in that, to make the board turn, you tilt the mast and sail from side to side rather than forward and back. However, the steering principle is still the same in that you tilt the sail in the opposite direction from where you want to turn. When you tilt the back of the booms closer to the water (A,B,C), you turn more upwind. When you tilt the front of the booms closer to the water (D,E,F,G), you steer more downwind. Note that as the back of the booms is tilted down and the board turns more upwind, it becomes necessary to trim the sail in to keep it from luffing (C). And when the front of the booms is tilted down and the board heads more downwind, you have to let the sail out to prevent overtrimming (F,G).

A

B

C

D

become your forward hand *(F)*.

The sail swings around in the wind to the opposite side of the board *(G)*.

Time to use your cross-over grip *(H)* and sail in the new direction *(I)*. Note that throughout this entire maneuver, while the board turns, the sail is kept square to the wind until the moment the rig is released and swung around to the opposite side. Holding the sail square to the wind is important in order to keep the board moving through the turn.

The Advanced Jibe

To begin an advanced jibe, steer more downwind by tilting the front of the booms toward the water (A,B).

As the board turns, continue to tilt the mast by extending your arms and shift your hips in the opposite direction. This gives you leverage to keep the sail from pulling you over (C,D). At the same time, pivot your feet to help push the tail of the board around.

Eventually you will turn far enough so that the wind is coming over the tail of the board and the rig is practically backward from the normal sailing position (E).

Now let go of the back of the booms with what has

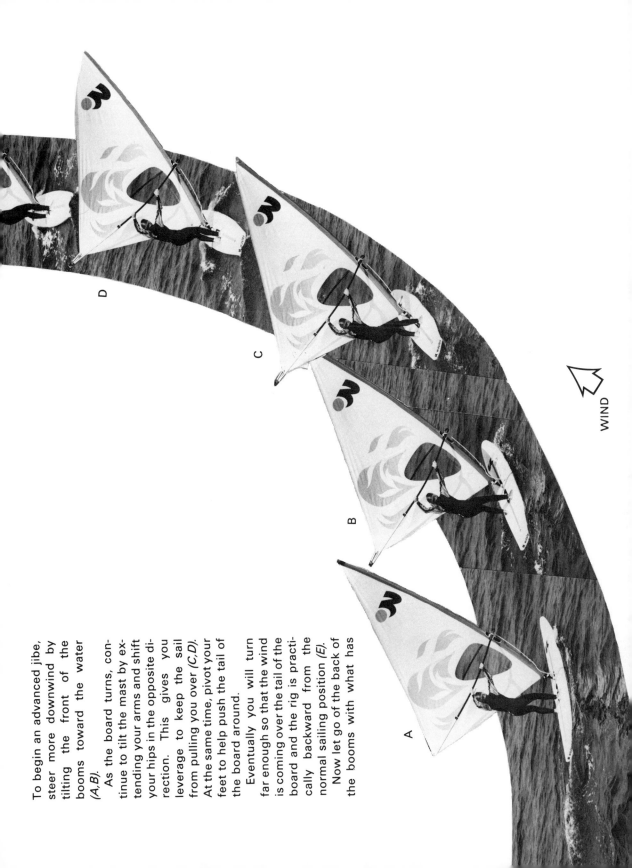

A

B

C

D

WIND

Foot, Shoulder and Hand Positions While Beating, Reaching and Running

When beating, the sail is closely trimmed.

When reaching, the sail is trimmed farther out.

When running, the sail is trimmed the farthest of all. As you move from a beat to a reach to a run, keep your feet parallel to the sail, which means turning them progressively more square to the centerline of the board.

of your body over the center of the board or even leaning slightly in the opposite direction.

Using this steering technique, it is easy to learn how to do a faster and more advanced type of jibe than a rope jibe. To begin, you tilt the rig toward the side of the board that the mast is closest to. The board will turn toward the opposite side, which will take it beyond directly downwind. If you tilt the rig to the wrong side, the board will start turning more upwind, which takes it away from jibing. Remember, you always turn *downwind* to jibe.

When the board turns far enough so that the wind is coming at an angle over the corner of the tail instead of from straight behind, let go of the boom with your back hand. Keep holding onto the boom with your other hand, but let the rig rotate freely in the wind. If you have turned the board far enough beyond straight downwind before letting go with your back hand, the sail will swing around the nose to the other side of the board. Quickly now, reach across and grab the other boom with your free hand, let go of the first boom with the other hand, grab the boom on the new side, and trim. It might seem a little complicated, but it is really quite similar to changing hands on a tack, except that the sail luffs less than when tacking, and you don't change from one side of the board to the other.

Transition Steering and Sheeting

Although it is important to learn to steer a straight course, it is also a good idea to practice steering in gradual curves upwind and downwind. In this way, you not only practice steering from one point of sail to another, but you also practice adjusting sail trim to coincide with the course changes. If you don't continually trim the sail in as you head upwind from a run, to a broad reach, to a reach, to a close reach, to a beat, it will luff and you will sail slower and slower as you turn. And if you don't gradually ease the sail out as you head progressively downwind from a beat to a run, you will be overtrimmed and out of balance.

The rule is that any time you head up, you automatically need to trim the sail at the same time. And any time you head down, you automatically ease the sail correspondingly. The more you head up, the more you trim in; the more you head down, the more you ease out. Thus steering by moving the sail forward or aft and sheeting by trimming or easing the sail become integral parts of the same maneuver, enabling you to maintain optimum sail trim to the course and wind direction at all times.

Your stance also needs to be adjusted from one point of sail to another. The easiest way to understand this is to remember that your feet and shoulders should be approximately square to your hands and the sail. Thus, as you head down from a beat, to a reach, to a run, the sail is gradually eased out, and your feet gradually change position. They go from (1) both being on the upwind side pointing across the board, to (2) the back foot being on the downwind side and the front foot on the upwind side, both pointing diagonally across the board, to (3) being next to each other on either side of the centerline pointing toward the nose. If you continually adjust your stance to keep your feet square to the sail as you change course, the shoulders will be square as well. And if the shoulders stay square, then you will be able to support the rig and trim the sail with the least amount of effort and the greatest stability.

Safety

Safety is something that should be a major concern throughout your boardsailing career, something you can't learn too early and something you never outgrow. We've already touched on such things as the importance of proper equipment, selecting the correct time and place to learn, and mastering one skill level before taking on the next. But at this point in your boardsailing development, safety becomes even more important.

You have just learned how to expand your boardsailing horizons, to increase your freedom and mobility, to go more places and do more things. And in the following chapter, you are going to learn how to move up to heavier winds, to go out in more challenging conditions, to sail on days when you previously would have sat and watched. This not only means that you are going to be in more situations that could, without the proper preparation and care, be potentially dangerous, but also, that you have probably outgrown some of the natural timidity with which you first entered the experience of learning to boardsail. Now more than ever, caution, common sense, and a sound knowledge of the rules of boardsailing safety are essential to becoming a competent, responsible boardsailor.

117

The best time to check equipment is before you go boardsailing—after may be too late.

KNOW YOUR LIMITATIONS

One of the attractions of boardsailing is the adventure of meeting new challenges. And it's true that you do get better by extending yourself. But at the same time, it is very important to know exactly what you can and can't handle. Develop your skills before you actually put them to the test. You don't want to find yourself out in 15 to 18 knots of wind and 4-foot seas when you still haven't mastered sailing downwind or have never sailed in anything more than a slight chop and an 8-knot breeze before. Self-confidence is great, but there is a point when it can be carried too far and become recklessness. Every boardsailor has his limitations, even the expert. Use your good judgment before you get yourself into a situation you can't easily get yourself out of. When in doubt, play it safe. Use a smaller sail, stick to the harbor instead of heading for open water, or even wait for more moderate seas or for the wind to die down some, or change to a more manageable and safer direction. And don't be swayed by others. The expert or advanced intermediate can make it look deceivingly easy out there in conditions that really are not that easy. Everyone has their own level of strength, technique, and experience. Know your level and what conditions you can handle.

AVOID SAILING ALONE

No matter how good you are or how much boardsailing experience you have, there are many times when it is foolish to sail alone. And for the learner, or even the intermediate who is still working on inconsistent skills, it should be a hard and fast rule never to sail alone. This is particularly true when sailing off an exposed shore or in any large, open body of water. You need to be certain that if anything goes wrong—a broken piece of equipment, an injury, inability to handle the conditions, fatigue—there is someone who can help you or can at least go for help. Until you reach a high level of competency, this is a rule you should stick to regardless of how small and protected the lake, or seemingly docile the conditions.

DON'T LEAVE YOUR BOARD

If you do find yourself in some kind of trouble that prevents you from sailing back to shore, never make the mistake of abandoning your board to swim for

safety. Your board is a personal flotation device. You can put a hole in it, even
break it in half, and it will still float you. No matter how strong a swimmer you
are, or how close the shore may look, you can never be certain that you won't
get tired or develop a cramp. Instead of swimming for shore, first try paddling.
Undo your outhaul, roll up your sail on the mast, and secure it and the booms
with the outhaul. Then with the mast extending back over the tail, you will be
able to paddle more effectively with minimum interference from the rig and sail.

Even if you find that you are getting blown out by an offshore wind, and
can't make any progress by paddling, resist the temptation to leave your board
and swim. You may want to make the decision to abandon your rig altogether,
if it appears that it will make your paddling easier. However, I would recommend that you hang onto your rig and, in fact, set it up again, even though this
can be an awkward task in rough water. Not only does the rigged sail act as
a sea anchor and slow your offshore progress, but also it is much easier for
rescuers to spot a sail lying in the water than just a board and sailor, and
certainly easier than a lone swimmer in the water.

USE A LEASH

Without a doubt, the most important piece of safety equipment in boardsailing
is the leash. This short piece of line insures that your rig doesn't become

This sailor remembered to use the safety
leash—the board and rig remain connected
even though the universal has popped out
after a fall. Since the sail now serves as a
sea anchor preventing the board from float-
ing away, all the sailor has to do is swim
back to the waiting board, climb on, put the
universal back in, and start sailing again.

Once a board gets away from the rig in strong winds or seas and there is no leash to keep them connected, a boardsailor faces one of the most potentially dangerous situations in boardsailing: being in the water, possibly far from shore, and without his board to float him. It is surprising and frightening how fast a board can be carried away from even a strong swimmer in heavy conditions.

separated from your board even if the universal pops out. This means that you still have the sea anchor effect of the rig to prevent your board from being carried away from you no matter how hard the wind is blowing or how large the waves are.

Unfortunately, far too many boardsailors don't take the five seconds needed to rig a leash, possibly thinking that their universal is in tight enough that it won't pop out or that even if it does, they will be able to catch the board before it gets very far away. Reasoning like this results in the all too common scene where a boardsailor surfaces after a particularly spectacular fall only to find that the board and rig have separated and that the board is already 10 yards away. In a 15-knot wind and two- to three-foot seas, it is unlikely that even a strong swimmer will be able to catch a board that is fast being carried away. What had been a slight inconvenience on the beach to set up a leash now becomes one of the most dangerous situations in boardsailing. Next time you're rigging up to go out, picture yourself in the water far from shore without your board. Almost all stock boards have provisions for a leash. If yours doesn't, get one. If it does, make sure you use it.

GUARD AGAINST HYPOTHERMIA

While hypothermia is not something that the average recreational boardsailor, especially the novice or intermediate, is likely to face very often, every boardsailor should be constantly aware of it as the most serious potential danger in boardsailing. Hypothermia occurs when the body temperature goes below 35 degrees centigrade. Caused by cold water, wind chill, and physical exertion, it produces shivering, loss of coordination, and, if not checked, loss of consciousness and even death.

Anyone who sails where the water stays relatively cold all year round or where the prevailing winds are consistently strong, or anyone who sails during the off-season, in the early spring, late fall, or winter, should constantly be on guard against hypothermia. But hypothermia can also be a threat to the summer, warm-water boardsailor who is not used to dealing with the cold and is not as likely to be prepared for keeping warm during a summer northerly or a sudden squall.

Regardless of where or when you sail, always be on the lookout for early symptoms of hypothermia, and if they appear, or if even the wind and temperature conditions that are likely to produce hypothermia develop, sail for shore immediately. Even in what seems like mild conditions, don't stay out on the water so long that you start to shiver or feel chills or reach a point of exhaustion where you begin losing your balance and strength and begin falling more frequently than normal. If for some reason you do get caught out on the water and can't get back in, conserve body heat by wrapping yourself in your sail, bringing your knees up to your chest, and hugging your legs.

The best rule is simply to dress warmly enough any time you go out on the water. A good wet suit is your most effective weapon against hypothermia. In most areas and conditions during the summer season, a farmer john or even just a shortie or a vest will provide adequate warmth and protection. But when it's cold and windy, you should have your arms and shoulders covered as well. And if it's late fall or early spring, you need further protection for your feet and head, both of which are extremely vulnerable to heat loss. When in doubt, overdress. It's better to be a little too warm than to find a half hour into your sail and a half mile from shore that you are suddenly cold and beginning to show some of the symptoms of hypothermia.

KNOW THE RIGHT-OF-WAY RULES

It's incorrect to think that the right-of-way rules are for racers only. As you get out and sail more with other boards and in other types of boat traffic, it is important to know the rules of the road, so that you can prevent unnecessary collisions. Nor is it sufficient to say that you will simply be careful to stay out of everyone's way. What the right-of-way rules do is specify whose responsibility it is to stay clear, so that both people don't turn the same way to avoid each other. In other words, only one person should have to change course to avoid a collision. The other person should continue steering a normal course so as not to cause any confusion.

Starboard over Port

The most frequently encountered right-of-way situation is two boards approaching each other on an intersecting course. The first method for determining who has the responsibility of staying clear is to see which hand is forward on the booms. If your right hand is forward on the booms, you are said to be on *starboard* and have right-of-way over someone who is on *port,* which you can tell if they have their left hand forward on the booms. In other words, if you are on starboard and an approaching board is on port, you inform the other sailor that you have the right-of-way by calling out "starboard." This means that you are going to hold your course and you expect him to alter his course to keep clear of you. This is the most basic of the right-of-way rules.

Closehauled over Offwind

But what if both boards are on starboard or both are on port? Who has the right-of-way then? When both sailors have the same hand forward on the boom, then the rule that applies is that the board that is the farther upwind of the two has the responsibility of staying clear. In other words, the board that is sailing more closehauled has the right-of-way over the board that is sailing more offwind. The downwind sailor calls "closehauled" in this situation to inform the upwind sailor of the need to keep clear. The logic behind this is that the sailor on the downwind board has his back to the upwind board and can't see to keep clear, whereas the sailor of the upwind board has a good view of the board he has to avoid.

Overtaking Keep Clear

Another important rule applies to when two boards are both on starboard or both on port and one is passing the other from behind. In this situation, the board that is doing the passing is obligated to stay clear, and the hail for right-of-way from the board being passed should be "overtaking board keep clear." One thing to keep in mind about these hails is that their purpose is simply to make sure that the other person is aware of your presence and the potential for a collision. You're not out on the freeway and demanding your rights in rush-hour traffic. You're out on the water enjoying yourself, and courtesy should be a constant consideration.

Sail over Power

The above rules not only apply to sailboards, but also to sailboats and any interaction between sailboards and sailboats. They are the rules for all sailing craft. As for interaction between sailing craft and powerboats, the rule is that sail has right-of-way over power. Even a sailboat that is under power must keep clear of one that is under sail. The reasoning behind this is that a powerboat has more maneuverability than a sailboat and is therefore better able to adjust course to avoid a collision.

However, even though this rule gives you right-of-way, a wise sailor never forces the issue. First of all, the consequences of being right, but having the powerboat either not know it or not care, are not worth it. And secondly, except possibly in extremely light air, no water craft, either sail or power, is as maneuverable as a sailboard. Granted, this depends greatly on the ability of the boardsailor, and you may have a strong case in arguing that you are not yet in control of the most maneuverable craft on the water. However, as you learn and improve, you will increasingly find that you are in the best position to keep clear in an emergency, which is the greatest benefit to your own safety.

Avoid Collisions at All Cost

This is the most important rule of all, and it has two main implications. It means that if you are obligated to keep clear in a situation, don't wait for the other person to say something. It's your responsibility to watch out for the right-of-way board and to keep clear whether he says something or not. On the other hand, whether you have the right-of-way or not, you should do everything in your power to prevent a collision with another board or boat. You will come across too many people who do not know the rules and their responsibilities and will return your hail for right-of-way with blank stares. It's irresponsible and dangerous for such people to be out on the water, but to stand on your rights and not make any effort to prevent a collision is even worse. Just remember, the ultimate purpose of the right-of-way rules is not legality; it's safety.

Rules of the Road

Starboard over Port

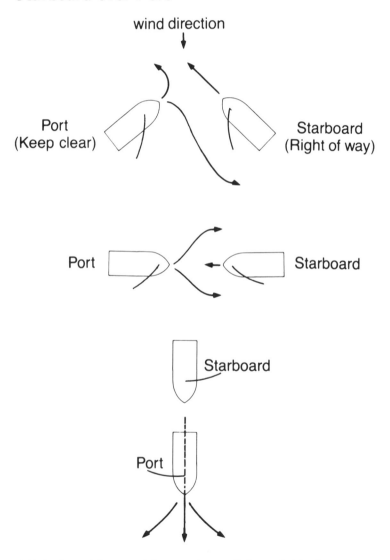

Right hand forward (toward mast) has right of way

Overtaking Keep Clear

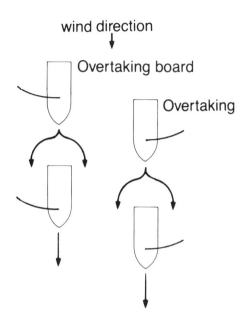

wind direction

Overtaking board

Overtaking

Closehauled over Offwind

wind direction

Less closehauled
(must keep clear)

More closehauled
(right of way)

Less closehauled

More closehauled

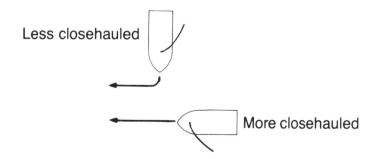

7

Moving Up to Stronger Winds

It's a big moment when a boardsailor takes that initial step to learn how to sail in stronger winds. Not only does this mean that you are moving from the ranks of the beginner to intermediate, but also, you are entering a whole new dimension of boardsailing. No longer will you have to sit on the beach every time the wind blows over 8 or 10 knots. And along with increasing your upper wind limit, you will also be increasing the scope of your speed, excitement, and fun. Light-to-moderate winds will always have their appeal, but once you have tasted the thrill and challenge of stronger winds, boardsailing will never be the same.

But before you can move up to stronger winds, be sure that all your basic skills are thoroughly developed. You can't learn how to tack and jibe one day and then take on heavy air the next. It's important to put in the necessary time on the board, practicing sail-trim and board-handling skills to the point that you are comfortable and confident on all points of sail and with all maneuvers in light-to-moderate conditions.

127

With a mastery of the basics, handling heavier air need not be a problem.

HEAVY-AIR EQUIPMENT

There are a few pieces of special equipment that can make it easier to learn to sail in strong winds. Perhaps the greatest aid is the marginal sail—the same marginal sail that made it easier to learn in light and moderate air. Having less than 55 square feet of area, a straight or hollowed leech, which is the back edge of the sail, and no battens to keep the leech stiff and powerful, a marginal sail allows you to get out in stronger winds without being overpowered and spending all your time in the water instead of learning. There are even times, especially for particularly small or light people, when the conditions may warrant using a 40-square-foot storm sail.

It's not just the reduced size that helps. With both the marginal and the storm sail, the area is mostly reduced toward the back of the sail, which means that it is better balanced in strong winds and less likely to round the board up into the wind. When in doubt, use the smaller sail. If you find you can handle the conditions too easily with it, you can always go back in and change. But if you go out with a sail that turns out to be too much for the conditions and your abilities, you may find it extremely difficult to get back in to change.

The other highly useful piece of heavy-air equipment is the *highwind centerboard*. This special centerboard comes in several different designs, but all are similar in two very important features. First, they all have reduced area, which allows the board to slip sideways slightly more in strong winds, reducing some of the pressure on the sail. This smaller size also limits the tendency of the centerboard to try to hydroplane to the surface at high speeds. This hydroplaning causes the board to tip up on its edge, which is called *railing*.

Some typical high-wind centerboard designs.

The second common characteristic is that highwind centerboards all have their area cocked or moved back toward the tail of the board, which moves the pivot point for turning farther back and thus makes it harder for the wind to round the board up. The only problem with using a highwind centerboard is that you will sideslip more and not be able to sail closehauled as effectively as with a standard centerboard. This means that you have to be careful about getting so far downwind that it becomes difficult to beat back upwind again.

MENTAL APPROACH

One of the keys to learning how to sail in stronger winds is the mental attitude you take into the experience. It is easy for people to be somewhat intimidated by heavy air—the speed, the spray, the sound of the wind. But there is really nothing to fear. As long as you stay away from open water, dress warmly, and don't sail alone, there is no real danger. You'll fall a lot, but after all, it's just water—and you should be used to that by now! Heavy-air boardsailing *is* more physical, but this doesn't mean that it requires significantly more physical strength. By far, the most important element is still technique.

Don't be timid. You can't really improve unless you're willing to take your share of the spills. Develop an aggressive, "I can do this" attitude. If you try to sail too cautiously, you will end up having more trouble learning than if you just go for it. Besides, you're not really doing anything differently from what you've done so far—pulling up the rig, trimming, tacking, jibing. You're merely building on what you've already learned, doing the same things, but modifying the techniques to handle the increased wind and speed. Just as when learning the basics, the secret is to concentrate on what you have to do instead of worrying about whether or not you can do it. It's a challenge and it's fun. Enjoy it and learn.

USING YOUR BODY

The biggest adjustment in sailing technique when moving up to heavier air is learning to counteract the increased wind strength. Even the strongest board-sailor can't do this on muscle alone. You need to learn how to use your body and your weight to balance the forces at work on the sail and the board.

The first thing you need to do is adjust your grip on the booms, moving your hands farther back to give yourself more leverage to trim the sail. Unless you make this adjustment, it becomes extremely difficult to keep the sail trimmed. And as you already know, if the sail is not kept trimmed, it luffs up

A   B

When the hands are too far forward on the boom in heavy air, as in *A*, there isn't enough leverage to trim the sail in sufficiently. As a result, the front of the sail luffs while the back of the sail fills with wind, pivoting the nose of the board more toward the wind *(B)*. This, in turn, causes even more of the front part of the sail to luff, and the board pivots even farther into the wind *(C)*. Finally, the board turns so far that the wind gets almost completely on the back side of the sail and actually forces

forward while the wind in the back rounds the board up into the wind and dumps the sailor in backward. This is an even bigger problem in heavy air, because the board rounds up so quickly that you seldom have time to recover before finding yourself in the water.

　　The other thing you need to do to combat this increased tendency to round up is *keep your front leg straight and your weight on the forward foot up next to the mast.* With this stance, you're in a better position to drive the nose back down when it tries to round up. Be careful not to make the common mistake of leaning back toward the tail when straightening your forward leg. This transfers the weight from the front foot to the back foot and actually helps the board round up, especially when the back foot has been moved even farther toward the tail to provide a wider stance for increased stability.

　　But the biggest problem in stronger winds is simply holding the rig up. It is impossible to stand in the same upright position you would use in lighter air, trim the sail, and not be pulled right over into the water. You need more leverage, and this is supplied by leaning back—sometimes falling back—just before trimming. In this way, your weight and gravity keep the sail from pulling you over, and the wind and the sail keep you from falling in backward. Also, as you lean back, the sail leans as well, which effectively reduces the sail area presented to the wind and makes it easier to keep from getting overpowered.

C D

the sailor backward and into the water *(D)*. Two techniques can help to curb this relatively common occurrence among novices facing heavy air: (1) moving the hands back on the boom creates more leverage to pull the sail in so that no part of it is luffing; (2) straightening the front leg applies some pressure to the front of the board to help keep it from rounding up into the wind.

At first it takes a certain amount of faith to start falling backward and believe that when you trim the sail it will stop you from ending up in the water. But after a while, you won't give it a second thought, like pushing off on a bicycle without the thought ever entering your mind that you might not be able to balance on those two skinny wheels. There really is a beautifully balanced interaction between you and the sail, your weight and the wind strength, the angle of your body and the effective sail area. You support the sail and the sail supports you.

As you've done previously with other new techniques, try this all out on the beach before trying it on the water. Just lean back and trim the sail to catch yourself. It takes a little practice to learn not to trim too soon or too late. But if you misjudge on dry land, you can step back to stop yourself from falling or just sit down in the sand. You will learn the timing and the balance more quickly this way because you don't spend so much time and effort climbing out of the water and pulling the rig back up.

Once you get the hang of trimming and can start sailing, the trick is to learn just how much lean is enough but not too much. This depends on the wind strength, the point of sail, and your size and weight. A light person sailing upwind in more than 18 knots of wind will need maximum leverage to keep from being overpowered and pulled over. To achieve this maximum leverage, you have your feet all the way out on the rail, your body perfectly straight, and your arms fully extended so that you can lean as far out over the water as possible. You also have the sail pulled over to reduce sail area as much as you can without taking away its ability to support you and keep you from falling in backward.

Falling Back and Trimming in Stronger Winds

A

B

Falling back and trimming in stronger winds. When first trimming to start sailing *(A)*, lean back as you sail *(B)*, so that when the sail is fully trimmed, your body has the leverage to keep you from being pulled over. Note here how Nancy Johnson has moved her hands back on the boom for more leverage to trim the sail against the increased wind. Note, too, how she straightens her front leg and transfers weight to her front foot to keep the nose of the board from rounding up into the wind.

A   B   C

If you trim the sail in without first leaning back for body leverage in stronger winds *(A)*, the increased strength of the wind in the sail pulls you right over *(B,C)*.

The best time and place to get the feel for falling back and trimming is in a moderate breeze on the beach. Experiment. Lean back and see how much leverage is enough to keep the sail from pulling you forward, yet not so much that the wind in the sail won't support you from falling over backward.

At the other end of the scale, a tall, heavy person sailing in 12 knots of wind would quickly find himself over backward in the water if he used the stance and body position described above. Instead, he would have to move his feet in closer to the centerline and, while he might still have his body straight, he would lean back only very slightly, keeping his arms bent and the rig upright for full power. Under these circumstances, leverage is not a problem. Keeping the weight over the board for balance is the main concern.

Another way to decrease leverage and increase balance is to keep the arms straight and the rig more upright, but to bend at the knees and the waist so that the pull is more down than out and the weight is kept more over the board. This is particularly good in shifty, puffy winds, because you can shift your weight so quickly between maximum and minimum leverage—simply by bending or straightening your legs to move in and out.

What do you do if you find that you do not have enough leverage, and the sail starts to pull you over? If the strength of the wind has pulled you upright or bent you forward at the waist, the best thing to do to save yourself from a swim, especially if you're just learning how to handle stronger winds, is simply to let go of the boom with your back hand. It's easier to trim and try it again than to start from scratch after a fall.

But if you're leaning out and the sail starts to straighten you up, this system won't work, since as soon as you let go with your back hand, you'll fall in backward. Instead, you ease out very quickly to give the sail just a brief luff that will let you lean back a little farther for more leverage. Then you immediately trim back in to keep yourself from falling back too far.

An effective variation on this technique is to luff briefly, bend your knees to drop your weight lower, and then straighten your legs as you trim again to push back out at an increased angle of lean. Too many boardsailors try to force themselves into a lower angle by pulling with their back muscles, which generally aren't strong enough to do the job and which usually end up pretty sore after an hour or so of effort. When you learn to luff momentarily and use your legs, you save your back.

But what do you do if, instead of not enough leverage, you have too much? What if you find yourself suddenly starting to fall in backward? If it's blowing really hard and you've got good speed, the easiest way to save yourself is to overtrim a little. By pulling in a little more with your back hand, you put more sideways pull on the sail, which makes it able to support more weight.

However, you have to be careful not to overtrim too much or for too long. When you overtrim, your forward motion is turned into sideways pull, and two things can happen. First, if you overtrim too far, the sideways force in the sail can increase so suddenly and radically that you can get pulled right over—from one extreme to the other. And second, if you overtrim for too long, especially in slightly more moderate winds, when your speed might not be quite as good to begin with, you begin sideslipping. This in turn reduces the pull in the sail and dumps you in backward.

The best method for recovering your balance in most conditions and circumstances is simply to bend your knees and move your weight in over the center of the board. As you've already learned, this pulls more down on the rig than out. Another way you can get your weight back in over the board and reduce outward pull is to bend your arms and/or arch your back and hips forward. By bending your arms, you pull yourself up closer to the boom in a position of less lean and leverage. And by arching your body, you get most of it in and pulling down even though the shoulders may still be leaning out.

HIGH-SPEED REACHING

Highwind reaching is one of the most exciting experiences in boardsailing. Most recreational boards, especially those with flat tail sections, were specifically designed for this point of sail and these conditions. And while most people tend to think that high speeds must be for the expert only, it is actually not particularly difficult to master the necessary techniques. Nor does it take great strength to handle the board and hold onto the rig. In fact, the faster you go, the less pressure there is on the sail.

The key to high-speed reaching is developing extremely fine balance techniques and quick reactions. Unlike beating in high winds, you seldom get overpowered when reaching. But when you're moving so fast, any error, even a very slight one, in body position or sail trim can become immediately magnified. This isn't to say that you don't still have to use your body for leverage. It's just that leverage isn't quite as important as when beating, and balance is a lot more important. You don't want to give up your leverage completely, but you want to be in a position to control it better.

The two main board control problems when reaching at high speeds are rounding up and railing up. If the board is slightly unbalanced, with one rail higher or lower than the other, it will steer off in one direction or the other. So if there is too much weight on the downwind rail, the board will swerve upwind. This can be a considerable problem, since the sail tends to try to round

How Much Leverage Is Enough?

The amount of leverage you need to hold up the rig depends on the strength of the wind and your height and weight. As the wind gets stronger, you need to move your weight gradually farther out over the water for more leverage and simultaneously to lean the sail more upwind to reduce its power.

A

B

In *A,* the wind is blowing at 5 knots. The body and the sail are both fairly upright, although the knees are bent slightly to put the sailor's weight just enough out over the water to keep him from being pulled over. Note that the sailor's feet are close to the centerline for stability. His arms are relatively straight to allow his body to get far enough out for the necessary leverage. Were the wind just a little lighter, the sailor's arms would be bent to bring his weight more in and over the board.

When the wind gets a little stronger (6 to 7 knots), it is necessary to move your weight farther out to balance the increased pull on the rig. In *B,* the sailor's legs are straight and the body is leaning back for increased leverage. This also causes the rig to lean slightly upwind, which decreases the pressure on the sail.

C

In even stronger winds (8 to 10 knots), the body needs to lean even farther out for leverage, and the sail leans even farther upwind to reduce power *(C)*. Notice that the sailor has moved his feet a little closer to the sail, both for more body reach and to prevent upwind railing.

D

Another way to gain good body leverage and stability in strong winds is to bend your knees and back, but to keep your arms very straight. In this way, you use maximum weight to hold the rig, but with less backward lean over the water *(D)*. Note how straight the rig is held in this stance.

Preventing a Forward Fall

A

B

If you don't lean out far enough in higher winds, the pull of the sail can bend you over at the waist, causing the mast to lean downwind, rob you of all your leverage, and begin pulling you into the water *(A)*. To save yourself from a swim: *(B)* quickly let the sail out with your back hand so that it luffs, spills wind,

C

D

and stops pulling you over; (C) straighten up at the waist and straighten the mast back up while the sail is still luffing; (D) let your body fall back into a position of leverage before trimming the sail again. When done properly, these three distinct steps form, in fact, one quick, smooth process.

do when beating. This position can become precariously difficult to control at high speeds. Instead, it's best to keep your knees and waist bent and to hang more from the booms in a manner that allows you to keep your weight low and more over the board. In this position, an error in steering or sail trim or even weight placement has less effect on your balance. This is because you are in a better position to keep your weight evenly balanced between your two feet and thus between the two rails. When you get a strong puff, with more pull from the sail and more of a tendency for the board to round up, you can easily shift your weight out. This not only provides more leverage, but also puts more weight on the upwind rail and more pressure on the forward foot, both of which help to prevent the board from rounding up.

Preventing a Backward Fall

B

A

D

C

If you have too much leverage for the strength of the wind and find yourself falling in backwards *(A),* you can recover your balance by quickly and momentarily overtrimming the sail *(B).* Notice that the end of the booms are well to windward of the centerline. This increases the sideways pull of the sail and actually lifts the sailor back up *(C)* into a balanced position, whereupon he continues sailing, his body and the rig in the proper position *(D).* Remember: this is a heavy air technique; lighter winds cannot lift the sailor's weight even with the sail overtrimmed.

A   B   C

Here, the sailor has overtrimmed too far and too long, causing the board to stop sailing forward and to slip sideways *(A,B,C)*. The pull of the sail is so dramatic that, after preventing the sailor's fall, it actually straightens her up and pulls her over forward. The sailor could have avoided a fall if, once she was pulled up by the rig, she let out the overtrimmed sail. This would have stopped the board from sideslipping, started it sailing forward again, and reduced the pull of the sail to a manageable limit. Note, too, that instead of letting go of the rig and falling safely away from the board, the sailor hangs on and falls against the board's nose *(D,E)*.

Since most railing takes place when the board rounds up and the upwind rail rolls up, you simply sail with a little more weight on the upwind rail to keep it down. However, you have to beware of overcompensating and putting too much weight on the upwind rail, which will cause the board to swerve downwind and the downwind rail to roll up. The trick is to keep the board as level as possible, adjusting your weight quickly from one rail to the other when the board begins to roll.

The best position for balance and control of the board is with your forward foot near the upwind rail and your back foot on the downwind side. The front foot is not quite as far forward as when beating, nor do the hands need to be quite as far back on the booms. And, of course, the feet and shoulders are square to the sail. Actually, because there is a far greater tendency for the board to swerve upwind and the upwind rail to lift than the opposite, the back foot should be placed with the heel on the centerline and the toes pointing diagonally toward the downwind rail. In this way, your weight is shifted a little more to the upwind side without taking away your ability still to balance the downwind rail by just putting more weight on the toes of your back foot.

As for body angle, you don't want to lean far out over the water, as you

D

E

In moderate conditions, the best way to recover your balance is to shift your weight in, more over the center of the board. Start by bending more at the knees *(A)*, arching your back and hips forward, and bending your arms to pull your upper body closer to the booms *(B)*. Finally, extend your arms again to get the mast upright and thus the sail at a better angle to support your weight when you return to correct body position *(C)*. Notice that when you are over-balanced to the upwind side (that is, you're leaning too far backward), the upwind rail (to the sailor's right in the photo), is forced down *(A)*, causing the board to steer downwind and making your balance even more precarious. By shifting your weight in, the downwind sail is forced down *(B)*, helping to steer the board back up and return it to a level plane and straight course.

A

B

C

High-Speed Reaching

High-speed reaching. The key to a good stance when high-speed reaching is stability. Because the board is moving so fast, the slightest imbalance becomes magnified. To achieve stability when reaching in heavy air, keep your weight as close over the board as possible while still maintaining leverage enough to keep the rig from pulling you over.

A

A well-balanced stance in more moderate winds. The sailor's weight is close to the centerline, yet his knees and arms are bent to provide enough leverage to keep the rig upright. Note, too, the sailor's feet are on either side of the centerline so that he can shift his weight quickly and easily from one side of the board to the other.

To counteract this railing, drop your weight even more—in this case mostly onto your front foot *(D)*—which balances the upwind rail. In this photograph, the sailor has applied a little too much leverage, as evidenced by the overly dropped upwind rail and by the upwind tilt of the mast.

D

B

As the wind increases, so does the need for leverage. This is applied, not by leaning back more as when beating, but by moving your rear out more while keeping your shoulders over the board for stability *(B)*. Note here how the sailor has shifted his hips forward to put more weight on his front foot. This keeps the board from rounding up.

C

As wind speed increases and more leverage and stability are needed, the body assumes even more of a "sitting" position *(C)*, which balances the rig with increased downward pull. Notice that the increased speed is causing the board to rail up on the upwind side.

E

The final adjustment to bring the board and rig back into trim comes from bending the knees even more, so that almost all of the weight is distributed over the feet *(E)*, and thus evenly balances the board. In this way, the sailor's legs control more of the body weight and the rig is returned to an upright position which is the position of maximum stability. As the wind picks up and the need for leverage returns, the sailor shifts his weight out more, off the legs, and onto the arms and thus the booms.

do when beating. This position can become precariously difficult to control at high speeds. Instead, it's best to keep your knees and waist bent and to hang more from the booms in a manner that allows you to keep your weight low and more over the board. In this position, an error in steering or sail trim or even weight placement has less effect on your balance. This is because you are in a better position to keep your weight evenly balanced between your two feet and thus between the two rails. When you get a strong puff, with more pull from the sail and more of a tendency for the board to round up, you can easily shift your weight out. This not only provides more leverage, but also puts more weight on the upwind rail and more pressure on the forward foot, both of which help to prevent the board from rounding up.

PULLING THE CENTERBOARD

Even when using proper high-speed reaching technique, it is sometimes too windy to keep the board from railing up—that is, turning up on its rail—especially when you are sailing in any kind of seas. If your board has a kickup or pivoting retractable centerboard, then you can maintain a certain amount of stability by placing the centerboard in the full-up position. But with a daggerboard, or even oftentimes with a kickup centerboard, the only way to keep the board under control is to pull the centerboard.

The reason pulling the centerboard gives you more control is that it removes the cause of both rounding up and railing up. You do initially lose a certain amount of stability that the centerboard provides in terms of dampening rolling. But once you get moving, the speed through the water makes the board surprisingly stable, easy to steer in a straight line, and completely free of any tendency to rail.

Because of the loss of stability from the time you pull the centerboard until you get moving, the key to executing this maneuver is to do it quickly and smoothly. It is best done starting out in a reaching position. You let go of the boom with your back hand, let the sail luff, reach down (bending at the knees more than the waist), grab the centerboard strap, pull the centerboard out (slipping your hand through the strap), lift your arm so that the centerboard slides up to your elbow, grab the boom, trim, and go.

The reason you don't bend just at the waist is that the rig either tilts downwind, invariably causing you to drop the sail in the water, or it tilts upwind and you both end up in the water. You want to reach down and pull the centerboard out with as little movement of the rig, the board, and your body as possible.

You might ask if it wouldn't be easier just to drop the rig, pull the centerboard, and then pull the rig back up. Because the board is less stable (when not moving) with the centerboard pulled, it is very difficult to lift the rig and keep your balance without it in. In fact, if you fall with the centerboard out, it is best to put it back in, lift the rig, and then pull it again before trimming.

It takes a little practice to trim in and get the board moving after you've pulled the centerboard. Because you slide sideways very easily without the centerboard in, it is important to get the board moving forward and to avoid stalling out. In other words, be careful not to overtrim or to try to bear off too quickly. Remember, there is no centerboard to pivot around, so you need some speed before you can turn. And even then, the board will turn much slower. If you do find yourself stalled and sliding sideways, let the sail luff, and when you stop sideslipping, reposition the board at right angles to the wind and try it again. With more experience, you will learn to stop the sideslipping and get the board moving without luffing the whole sail, but when first learning, it is easier just to sheet out and start over.

One final point: Because there is more sideslipping with the centerboard out, you can't sail upwind with it pulled. This technique is for reaching, although it can often be helpful when running as well. So when you want to go upwind and have to put the centerboard back in, you just reverse the process of taking it out. On the other hand, if you don't feel like hassling with all that balancing, you can always drop the rig, replace the centerboard, pull the rig up again, and head upwind.

SAILING DOWNWIND

Surprisingly enough, the most difficult point of sail to master in stronger winds is running. This may seem contrary to earlier learning experiences when it appeared that it was almost too easy to end up way downwind, facing difficulties getting back upwind. But the heavy-air learner generally finds that he can get upwind. It's getting back downwind without spending most of the time in the water that's the problem. This is because, when running in stronger winds, the sail does not offer the stability that it does when beating and reaching. You cannot really lean back against the pull of the sail for support, and your stance puts you on the narrowest, most unstable axis of the board. This doesn't mean that sailing downwind in a breeze is not fun or that only an expert can do it. It just means that it requires a definite technique and takes a little practice.

Pulling the Centerboard

A

It's best to pull out your centerboard with
the board in a beam-reach position (A).

B

Let the sail luff free by releasing the boom
with your back hand and holding the rig
up with your forward hand still on the
booms (B).

C

Reach down for the centerboard with your back hand, bending at the knees and the waist *(C)*. Note: bending at the waist alone makes it impossible to hold the rig up and keep the sail out of the water and luffing free.

D

Now pull the centerboard from its slot and straighten up *(D)*.

Pulling the Centerboard (Cont.)

E

As you straighten, slip your hand through the centerboard strap so that it slides up to your elbow (E).

F

With the centerboard hanging in this position, it is easy to grab the boom again with the back hand, trim, and resume sailing (F).

The challenge of sailing downwind in heavy air begins with simply trying to get headed downwind in the first place. You can't just luff your sail in a downwind position and then try to trim and get going. It takes expert technique to do this without falling, rounding up, or dropping the rig. Instead, you start out sailing on a reach, which is not difficult to get to from either a luffing position or a beat, and then head down onto a run. The challenge is in getting the board to head down in conditions where it has a natural tendency to head up.

The first step is to luff very slightly and very briefly to slow down some. Immediately, you lean the mast forward and upwind. At the same time, your front foot is moved forward and out where it can both push the nose downwind and sink the upwind rail. All of these things act together to get the board to steer down. Now come the key steps that make the difference between successfully getting headed downwind and ending up in the water. As the board gradually heads down, you have to do three things: (1) you have to bring your weight back in; (2) you have to pull the mast back; and (3) you have to let the sail out.

As you go from a reach to a broad reach and from a broad reach to a run, the rig offers less and less support to your weight, which means that you cannot remain leaning out without falling in the water. In fact, as soon as the board begins turning, you should begin bending your back leg to move your weight gradually back in over the board, finally ending up with your body in approximately the correct balance position for running by the time the board ends up on a run. The only other thing you have to do with your body is bring your front foot back part way when you get onto a broad reach and then all the way back parallel to your rear foot when you get onto a run.

The adjustment of the rig and sail during this maneuver coincides very neatly with your weight adjustment. As you move your weight back, you automatically pull the mast back, which not only helps steer the nose downwind, but also progressively places the rig in the correct position for broad reaching and then for running. At the same time, pulling the mast back helps to ease the sail out gradually. Next to not moving one's weight in, failure to let the sail out is probably the greatest cause of falls when trying to head down. Unless the sail is kept square to the wind as the board turns, you end up badly overtrimmed, with the whole rig out of balance and the board trying to round up.

Sailing Downwind in Heavier Air

Perhaps the most difficult part of sailing downwind in stronger winds is getting headed off onto a downwind course in the first place. Since pointing the board's nose downwind and trimming are extremely difficult, instead you should sail a course from beating to reaching to running *(A)*. First, let the sail luff for a moment to slow the board slightly *(B)*. Then, move your rear foot back and to the downwind side of the centerline, and your front foot forward *(C)*. Now, when you tilt the rig forward to head off, you can apply your weight to the front foot, which helps keep the upwind sail down and also helps push the nose downwind *(C,D)*. In order to have enough leverage to hold the sail up while doing this, you must also lean slightly out and drop your weight down *(C)*. Then, as the board heads gradually downwind and the need for stability gradually replaces the need for leverage, rotate your weight off your front foot and balance it over both feet until you finally can bring your right foot to its downwind position *(D,E)*. It is also important, while the board is turning and you're shifting your weight, to let the sail out with your back hand and simultaneously to pull the mast around with your front hand so that you are not over-trimmed when you end up on your downwind course.

A

B

C

D

E

Balancing Downwind

Once you've successfully headed off and are actually sailing downwind, the key to balancing is to keep the rig up and over the board, and to keep the board level and under you. Since you can't really lean back against the pull of the sail the way you can when beating and reaching, you get your leverage to keep the rig up and to keep from being pulled over the nose by standing farther back on the board and by keeping your arms bent. This also tilts the rig back, depowering the sail by reducing the effective area. And by keeping your arms bent, you provide a shock absorber that allows you to give a little in a hard puff so that you aren't immediately pulled off balance. Another key is to keep your legs bent without leaning forward at the waist. Remember, once you let your shoulders get forward of your knees, you lose all your leverage and are forced to pull with your back instead of your legs.

Lateral balance also depends on bending the legs. The challenge is to try to keep the board level, not only to make balancing easier, but also so that the board won't constantly be swerving off to one side or the other. But you can't

This is a relatively precarious downwind stance. True, the sailor's shoulders are behind the knees, allowing some leverage to hold the rig up, but not much. With the mast leaning forward, the body bent at the waist, the arms extended instead of bent, and the feet too far forward on the board, it would take only a slight increase in wind strength to overpower the sailor.

Increased leverage

To achieve sufficient leverage downwind in heavy air, lean the mast back toward the tail so that the sail is depowered. Stand slightly farther back on the board than normal (but not so far back that the board becomes unstable) and bend your arms at the elbows in order to keep the booms close to the body. If the wind increases significantly, bend at the knees and drop into a semisitting position for maximum leverage.

do this effectively by consciously putting your weight on one rail or the other. If you do, the result invariably is that you overbalance and actually induce rolling more than you dampen it.

The best way to shift your weight from side to side without overbalancing is simply to bend your knees, much the way a skier does when weighting or unweighting a ski. Bending one knee automatically shifts the weight off of that foot and onto the opposite foot. It's fast, efficient, controllable, and becomes instinctive with just a little practice. When the board rolls one way, you just bend the opposite knee to balance it. One additional advantage with this technique is that most of your body and the rig stay over the center of the board for maximum stability.

The other safeguard against overbalancing is to keep the feet relatively close to the centerline. While you would think that a wider stance would be more stable, having your feet too close to the rails is actually one of the main causes of overbalancing. Not only does it give you too much leverage, but you

Improper Balance Technique
for Sailing Downwind

D

C

When balancing laterally downwind, it is important neither to be stiff nor to overbalance. In this sequence, the potential for overbalancing is already present in the position of the sailor's right foot—it is too far out toward the rail—and in the stance, which is too upright and stiff, especially in the hips and torso. As a result, there is too much weight on the left foot (A), and the sinking of the left rail is likely to be

B

A

corrected by too much pressure on the right foot, causing the board to roll to the right *(B)*. Finally, so much weight is put on the left foot to stop the roll *(C)* that the overcorrection puts the left rail too far down into the water, and the sailor becomes hopelessly off balance *(D)*.

Keep center of sail over center of board

A

Proper Balance Technique for Sailing Downwind

Instead of consciously shifting weight to one foot or one side, the proper technique for balancing downwind requires small and subtle weight adjustments. By bending one knee or the other and shifting your hips in the same direction, you can make the necessary balance adjustments to board trim.

In this sequence, the sailor's movements are slightly exaggerated due to the waves, but in essence, he bends his left knee to transfer weight to his straight right leg and simultaneously shifts his hips left to balance the weight on the right side of the centerline. In addition, he moves his shoulders and the rig in the direction of the weight foot *(A)*.

To shift his weight back to the opposite side, the sailor bends his right knee, and shifts his hips to the right and the shoulder and the rig to the left *(B)*. In effect, the upper and lower body move independently of each other, allowing fine board trim adjustments and good stability and balance. This technique becomes even more important later when you start sailing downwind in bigger waves and find yourself making more adjustments.

B

also end up having to shift your weight so far from one side to the other that it slows down your reactions and makes it harder to control your movements. By keeping your feet more toward the center of the board, it actually forces you to use just your knees instead of your whole body.

Even after learning all the proper techniques for sailing downwind, you may sometimes find yourself out in wind and sea conditions that you can handle upwind, but haven't quite mastered downwind. If you find yourself in such a situation, you can always get safely back downwind simply by holding onto the boom handle and letting the sail weathervane out over the nose of the board. You'll be surprised at how fast you can sail downwind with the sail luffing. You hold the rig with one hand, balance with your free arm, bend slightly at the knees, let the mast lean slightly forward for support, and steer as you would doing a rope turn, by merely tilting the mast to one side or the other.

Even when conditions become overpowering, you can always get back downwind merely by letting the rig and sail weathervane over the nose of the board. Notice that the stance is the same as if you had trimmed and were sailing. To steer, tilt the mast to one side or the other, as if you were doing a rope turn.

Sailing in Waves

In most places where people boardsail, it's unusual to have a significant increase in wind strength without also having some increase in the roughness of the water. On small inland lakes or in protected coves or harbors, this might be nothing more than a short, close chop. In open water areas, on the other hand, more wind generally brings real waves. It's all relative. But what it means is that, once you've reached the intermediate level and are beginning to develop your skills further, you have to learn to sail in waves to be able to enjoy some of the best boardsailing conditions.

I'm not talking about eight-foot breaking surf like that you find in Hawaii. Just plain old rough water can be challenge and excitement enough for the boardsailor who has spent his whole learning stage seeking out flat-water conditions. But it's not difficult to adapt to chop or waves if you have strong fundamental skills and have learned the techniques of moving up to heavy air. Boardsailing in seas is just a matter of being able to cope with another balance variable.

161

Waves present the boardsailor with one of his biggest challenges.

GETTING OFF THE BEACH

Unless you're in a protected area, to sail in waves, you normally have to launch through waves. But when learning the basic wave-launching techniques, you are better off starting in relatively mild conditions. This means using some good judgment and common sense in choosing not to try to negotiate three- to four-foot waves that are closing out (or breaking) five yards offshore. It also means considering the replacement cost of potentially broken masts and booms resulting from a fall in the surf. Beware especially of days when the wind is blowing straight onshore, forcing you to beat out through the waves at a bad angle. Also beware of days when the waves are stronger than the wind, and you can't get enough speed to get through them. First you lose your momentum, then your balance, and then your board and rig. In the beginning you should learn the proper techniques without the constant threat of costly wipeouts.

In preparing to launch, you need to make sure that everything is ready to start sailing *before* you leave the beach. In other words, the rig and leash should already be attached to the board, and if you have a kickup centerboard, it should be in place and kicked up. It should be said that, while there are advantages and disadvantages to both kickup centerboards and daggerboards, the kickup type makes it much easier to launch off a beach, especially in waves. With a daggerboard, you either have to be expert enough to sail out through the waves into deeper water carrying it over your arm, or you have to fight the waves to pull the board out into water deep enough to put the daggerboard in before sailing. If your board will only take a daggerboard, then use a highwind one that is shallow enough to be put in place before launching.

When you're ready, point the nose of the board out toward the water and stand next to the tail on the upwind side. Then pick up the board at the base of the skeg with your back hand, while holding the rig and luffing sail by the mast or boom handle with your forward hand. From this position you are ready to push the board out into the water, get on it, trim, and start sailing in the least amount of time and without having to pull the sail out of the water with the uphaul. This is extremely important. Not only is it next to impossible to stand on the board in breaking waves to pull the sail up, but there is also a potential for damage to your equipment any time your rig is down in the surf.

As you stand poised at the water's edge, watch the approaching waves for a slight lull, a set that isn't quite as large as the rest. Try to spot it as far away from shore as possible so that you have time to get out into the water and be ready when it gets there. When you spot your set, push out, keeping the nose directly into the waves so that it won't get washed to one side or the other. It is also helpful to keep the board cocked at an angle on its rail so that it will slice through the waves better while you're holding it. The rig and sail should be held up out of the water. Unless the wind is blowing from a strange angle or there is not very much wind, the breeze should help lift the sail, much in the same way it does when you carry it over your head on shore.

When the set of smaller waves reaches you, turn the nose so that the board is pointing well out of the wind, since it will try to round up as soon as you release the tail. When the tail is dropped, immediately grab the boom and partially trim the sail. This continues to keep the rig up out of the water and also allows you to use the rig to keep the board pointing the direction you want it to, just as if you were steering it. But don't hesitate any longer than you absolutely have to in this position. No lull lasts for too long, and even with a certain amount of control over the board, a larger wave can easily spin it around or wash it away.

So as soon as you can, after dropping the tail and partially trimming the sail, you should place your back foot on the board and trim the sail the rest of the way to help you step up onto the board with your front foot and get sailing immediately. In this way, there is no hesitation period during which you have to balance in the waves while trying to trim and get moving. From the moment you are fully on the board, the sail is trimmed and offering stability. For all practical purposes, you are already sailing.

It does take a little practice to learn just how far and how fast you need to trim. Too much or too fast and the sail can pull you over. Too little or too slow and there's not enough pull to help you up onto the board. Also, once you put your back foot on the board, you have to trim and make your move right away. Otherwise, the weight of your foot on the back of the board will pivot it up into the wind.

Speed is the key to making it out through the section of breaking waves that usually extends a certain distance off the shore, depending on the wind strength and the contour of the bottom. This means you need to gain as much speed as possible between waves, even heading down for more speed if necessary. It also means you should head up slightly into a wave so that you slice straight through it rather than end up sideways to it and be capsized or washed back toward shore. Also, try to time your move so that you don't sail through a wave right where it is breaking. Try to sail through the white water *after* it breaks or get to it *before* it breaks, while it is still rolling. Once you get past this section of breaking waves, the seas farther out will be much easier to handle.

A

Launching in Waves

When launching in waves, preparation is the key. Make sure everything is ready before you push off from shore, and understand that the way you launch needs to be just "one step away" from actually being on the board, trimmed, and sailing. Thus, start on the upwind side of the board with your forward hand supporting the rig and your back arm supporting the board at the tail *(A)*.

B

In this manner, you can push the board forward, letting the wind help support the sail and rig *(B)*.

C

At the water's edge, pause momentarily to find a "flat spot" in the waves *(C)*.

Then enter the water, being careful to
direct the nose of the board straight
into the waves so that the board is not
washed to one side or the other *(D,E)*.

D

E

Finally, when you're ready to get on
and trim, turn the nose of the board
well out of the wind—at least to a
beam reaching course and ideally
broader *(F)*. If, instead, you drop the
board and try to step on and trim
when it is pointed too close to the
wind, it will round up into the wind,
and likely dump you.

F

A

Launching in Waves (Cont.)

As soon as you drop the tail of the board, grab the boom with your free back hand in its proper trimming position *(A)*.

At this point, if the waves are not too large, you actually can steer the board straight into the waves (so that it won't get washed to either side) by partially trimming the sail with your back hand and either pushing down or easing up on the mast with your forward hand *(B)*.

B

By keeping the sail partially trimmed and pushing down (and downwind) on the mast, you can get the nose of the board to steer downwind into proper position for your stepping aboard. The trick here is not to trim too much (since this will make the board try to sail away from you), or too little (since there will not be enough wind force to steer the board or help support the rig [*C*]).

C

If you do fall in waves that are breaking, it is important to do two things as quickly as possible, ideally before the next wave hits. First, grab the mast close to the tip. Second, get up-wave of the board, taking the mast with you. You definitely don't want to be in any kind of a position where a wave can throw the board into you, so don't get between the board and the shore. You also don't want to have the rig between the board and shore, since a wave can push the board back onto it and break the mast or booms. All you really have to do is grab the mast, pull it off to the side, and lift the tip out of the water before the next wave hits. The wave will push the board harmlessly inshore while you hold the mast. In this manner, you can work your way back to shore, pull the board out of the water, get everything set up again, and give it another try. Not unless the waves are harmlessly small should you attempt to climb back on the board and try to pull up the sail after a fall in surf.

BALANCING IN WAVES

Once you get out—and be patient, you will—the main thing to keep in mind about waves that will help you learn to boardsail in them is that there is almost always a fairly defined pattern and rhythm to them. If you can accustom yourself to the pattern so that your body and movements can pick up the rhythm, you will be able automatically to react and adjust to the wave action.

For instance, it is always important to be aware, consciously or unconsciously, of where you are on a wave at any given time. Are you in the trough or on the crest, on the back side or the face? If you are on the face, the wave will roll you in the direction it is moving. If you are on the back, you will roll away from the direction the wave is going. Thus, from a relatively flat, stable, position in the trough between two waves, the approaching wave will roll you first forward and then back in the opposite direction after it lifts you and passes underneath.

When you are beating, you are usually sailing at an angle into the waves, since most of the time the wind and waves are coming from about the same direction. Thus you bend your knees slightly to absorb the shock as you come up the face of the wave and then straighten again as you head down into the trough. This "unweighting" and "weighting" is similar to skiing bumps and moguls, but not as pronounced. When you are sideways to the waves, either

Launching in Waves
(Conclusion)

If the waves are large or if you are not yet expert at steering the board into the waves using the rig and sail, you should plan on stepping onto the board as soon as you have dropped the tail and before the next wave can wash the board away. There are several key points to this technique of "stepping on" to keep in mind.

A   B   C

First, keep the sail trimmed (A). It is the wind in the sail that helps to lift you onto the board. For this reason, as you are stepping up on the board with your back foot, you should extend your arms in order to lift the sail as high as possible into the wind for maximum power (B,C). The moment your back foot is on the board, lift your body and front foot up, using the lift the sail provides, and also pulling down on the boom with your front arm (C,D).(Too much pull with the back arm will overtrim the sail and rob you of the power needed to help lift you.)

D   E

Once completely on the board, let the sail luff slightly so it doesn't pull you over and position your weight over the centerline *(D)*. Quickly balanced, you can finish trimming and be sailing within seconds of first stepping on the board *(E)*.

pulling up the sail, trimming, or sailing, balancing is a matter of moving your weight in or out to react to what the wave is doing and to anticipate what the wave is going to do next. On the face of a wave, you have to move your weight out to counteract the board being rolled forward down-wave and downwind. On the back of a wave, you have to shift your weight back in to balance the board rolling backward, up-wave and upwind.

The key is to react *and* anticipate at the same time. It is all too common, when the board is rolled forward by the face of a wave, for some to lean back to counteract the roll, and to fall in backward when the wave passes underneath and the board rolls in the other direction. When you're in the trough, you need to anticipate the forward roll and begin adjusting your weight the instant it begins. Then when you reach the crest, you should already be moving your weight back toward the centerline in anticipation of being rolled in the opposite direction on the back of the wave.

If you can keep your knees bent and your body relaxed, you can learn to shift your weight quickly and smoothly without actually leaning your whole body in one direction or the other. In fact, using this stance, you will be able to develop the ability to shift your weight instinctively, without even having to think about where you are on the wave. This is extremely important when reaching. Everything happens so fast. Plus, the rolling is magnified by the board trying to steer in the direction of the roll and then rail up.

However, the trickiest point of sailing in waves is running. This is partly because running is such a difficult point of sail on which to maintain balance in the first place, but it's also because waves coming from behind are the most unpredictable. It is difficult to tell in which direction you will roll or in which direction the waves will try to steer you. Again, the best stance is with the knees slightly bent and the body relaxed, so that you can shift your weight front and back or side to side simply by moving the hips and knees. If the wave is coming directly from behind, it is a little easier to keep the board level and steer straight. But if a wave is coming a little bit from one side—for instance, the upwind side —it will first hit the tail and try to steer you upwind. Then it will hit the nose and try to steer you downwind. In addition, it will first roll you forward and then back. Just as when you are sideways to the wave, you have to react and anticipate simultaneously so that you don't overbalance or oversteer and end up even more off balance.

The final thing you have to be concerned about when balancing in waves is keeping the nose from burying itself into the wave in front of it. This is not such a big problem when sailing upwind. Bending and straightening your legs

If you fall in waves that are breaking and that might damage your equipment or harm you, quickly grab the mast and move away from between the board and shore *(A)*.

A

Falling in Waves That Are Breaking

Then hold the mast up so that there is less chance of a wave breaking on top of the sail and rig *(B)*.

B

The conditions in these photos are actually mild enough to allow the sailor to get back on the board and pull up the rig. In rough seas close to shore, it is usually best to guide the board back to shore and start over again *(C)*.

C

A   B

When balancing in waves, you must not only react quickly and smoothly to what the wave is doing to you, you must also anticipate what it will do next. In this very common sequence of events, the sailor reacts too late to the upwind rail being lifted by the face of a wave. She leans back to counteract the lifting rail *(A)*, but because

to unweight and weight will help you to get over waves without too much trouble. And even if you do bury the nose, seldom are you not able to punch through the wave. But when you are sailing downwind, burying your nose into the wave in front of you usually means that the board suddenly stops and you and the rig keep going. Keeping your weight toward the back of the board will help keep the nose up and out of the waves, but you can only move so far back before the board begins to get more unstable. At this point you simply have to try to slow down so that you don't sail into the wave in front of you. Or you can steer a little to one side or the other so that if you do sail into a wave from behind, you will hit it at an angle rather than put your nose directly into it.

LANDING

After you've gotten off the shore in waves, getting back in again is nowhere near as tricky, so long as you keep a few important things in mind. The most important is that the greatest danger when landing in waves is either burying

C

she is late, she overcorrects and is not ready to change her balance once the crest of the wave passes beneath. Thus when the back side of the wave lifts the downwind rail of the board and the upwind rail tilts down, the sailor is caught leaning out too far to shift her weight in and recover *(B)* and is dumped in backward *(C)*.

the nose in the steep shore break and being thrown in front of the board, or having a wave break over you from behind and wash you off the board. The best way of avoiding these two problems is to position yourself just behind the wave in front of you. In this way, you are far enough ahead of the following wave not to be affected when it breaks. At the same time, by being careful to keep your speed down, you keep from driving your nose into the wave ahead.

As you begin to approach the stretch of breaking waves, pick a wave and sail up to the back of it, luffing intermittently to slow down as you get closer. Then when you get to the wave, you can trim just enough to keep up with it, but not so much that you sail through it. Actually, as long as you keep your weight back a little on the board, forcing the nose up slightly, it is very difficult to sail through a wave ahead of you. Instead, you sort of pin yourself against the back of the wave. It is only when you approach the wave with speed that you are in any real danger of burying the nose. Another technique for attaching yourself to the back of a wave is to slow just outside the breaking area and let the wave behind pass underneath you. Then you immediately speed up again to stay on the back of it. When the wave breaks, it will do so harmlessly in front of you.

Balancing When Running Downwind in Waves

The reason that balancing downwind in waves is so difficult is that when you begin to surf or accelerate on the face of a wave, any imbalance in board trim is magnified. In this sequence, the sailor is already leaning forward at the waist when the wave behind him begins to lift the board's tail *(A)*. When the board begins to accelerate on the wave's face, both sailor and rig are thrown off balance. The sailor responds by arching his back to keep his weight centered and by straightening his left leg, which sinks the upwind sail and causes the board to steer offwind *(B)*. Then, to recover his balance and original course, he bends his knees, moving his weight to the opposite rail, tilts the rig, and trims the sail, all of which head him back up *(C)*. Unfortunately, these corrections are magnified by the effect of the wave, turning them into overcorrections. Thus, as the board heads back up, it accelerates even more on the wave and, because the sailor's weight is on the downwind side of the board, the upwind side rails up uncontrollably *(D)*, and finally dumps the sailor and the rig irrevocably off balance *(E)*.

WIND

A

B

C

D

E

A   B   C

Landing in Waves

When landing in waves, it is a good idea to position yourself on the backside of a wave so that you are in no danger of accelerating and burying your board's nose in the wave ahead *(A)*. If you find you are in danger of starting to surf on too steep a wave, or are going to bury your board's nose, let your sail luff momentarily and then trim again to follow the wave in *(B)*. When you reach shallow water close to shore, quickly step off the board with your front foot and continue partially trimming the sail to help give you support *(C)*. As soon as your front foot hits bottom, release the

F

D   E

booms with your rear hand and step off with your rear foot *(D)*. Still holding the rig up with your front hand so that the wind will keep the sail out of the water, grab the far rail *(E)*, and pull the board up on edge. In this way, you can control the board and prevent it from being washed ashore even when the wave behind finally reaches you *(F)*. Now push the board ashore in the same manner you launched it—on its rail *(G)*. Once on land, still holding the board by the rail, keep the sail up in the wind and turn the nose of the board into the wind before laying the rig down *(H)*.

G   H

A B C

Securing the Rig

A quick, efficient method for securing the rig is, first, to roll up the sail along its back edge *(A,B)*. Lay the booms (still attached at the inhaul) parallel to the mast and rolled sail. Then wrap the outhaul around the mast and sail, first at the end of the booms *(C)* . . .

When you're close enough to shore, you quickly jump off the board on the upwind side, letting go of the sail with your back hand, but still holding onto the boom or onto the mast with the front hand. Then you pick up the tail of the board at the base of the skeg with your free hand before the next line of white water reaches you. This is the same position you used for launching, and it allows you to keep the board under control instead of having the waves wash it up onto the shore. Even if the shoreline is sandy beach, it is best for your equipment to turn the board around after the wave has passed and pull it ashore on its rail.

D   E   F

. . . and then up near the outhaul cleat *(D)*. Secure the outhaul to the outhaul cleat *(E)*. Then wrap the uphaul around the mast and sail, from the boom handle toward the universal *(F)*.

The sail is now lashed securely to the mast and the mast tied to the booms so that the booms serve as a convenient handle for carrying the entire rig *(G)*.

G

Using a Harness

The harness is the greatest invention since the introduction of boardsailing itself. With it, you can sail farther, for longer periods, in stronger winds, and with less effort. The harness is the great equalizer. It allows the 110-pound woman to get out and sail in heavy air with the 160-pound man. Nor is it difficult to learn to use the harness. The techniques are straightforward and closely related to the skills you have already learned. Try them out first on land and then in steady winds that are not overpowering, but strong enough to require you to lean back to balance the rig. You'll find that the harness can put the recreation back into heavy-air recreational boardsailing.

HARNESS EQUIPMENT

The boardsailing harness is a device that allows the body to be connected to the booms so that the arms don't have to do all the work of supporting the rig and the sailor's weight. Basically, it is just a piece of material, kind of a brief jacket, that is worn on the upper body to which is attached a hook. This hook is what connects to 3-foot lengths of line called harness lines. These are fastened to

181

The harness, which helps the arms support both the rig and the sailor's weight, makes distance and heavy-air sailing a breeze.

the booms by means of harness line straps, which either tie around the boom or are secured with Velcro-type material.

The harness itself comes in all shapes, sizes, and styles. There are brief, high-back harnesses that are lightweight and provide maximum freedom of movement. There are low-back harnesses that are almost like short-sleeve jackets and that provide maximum support. Harnesses come with plastic hooks and metal hooks.. They have pouches and pockets on the back for carrying things. You can even get harnesses that double as life jackets. But regardless

A

Harnesses, Backview

On the left, a standard-length harness with a side-access carrying pouch *(A)*. On the right, a low-back harness (for added support) with top-access pouch.

The hooks *(B)* are attached to the harness by means of straps that run from the sides and from the shoulders. While most boardsailors prefer wearing the hook in the down position, some choose to wear the hook facing up. In either case, the hook is the critical contact point between the harness/sailor and the harness lines/rig.

B

of the kind you buy, it should fit comfortably, without chafing the shoulders
or putting excessive pressure on the ribs. It should also have a quick-release
device in case you need to get out of it in a hurry.

SETTING UP

There are really only two things that you have to set up when using a harness
—the hook and the lines. The hook can be worn either up or down without
appreciably affecting performance. This choice is mostly just a matter of personal preference and what you get used to, although most recreational boardsailors seem to prefer using the hook down.

Attaching the Harness Lines

The harness lines are attached to the
booms by means of harness straps *(A),*
which are secured in this case by a
hook-and-fleece-type material. With
harness lines on both booms, the
boardsailor has something to hook into
and lean his weight against regardless
of which side of the board or rig he is
on *(B)*.

A

B

How you set up the harness line is a lot more crucial. In fact, the single biggest obstacle to learning how to use a harness correctly is having the lines set up in the wrong position. Unfortunately, since everyone is different, there is no set of standard measurements you can use. Instead, think in terms of positioning the lines so that they lead from where you would normally have your hands. After all, the harness and lines are supposed to do the work for the arms. If your hands are positioned to provide a comfortable, evenly balanced pull, then the harness lines should provide equal comfort and balance when set up in the same position.

The most common mistake is for someone to set their harness lines up too far forward and then find that the sail won't stay trimmed and that the board is constantly rounding up and dumping them in backward. Remember when you first moved up to stronger winds that you had to move your grip back on the booms to be able to keep the sail properly trimmed in far enough. If just your weight in the harness won't keep the sail trimmed, if you are forced to pull hard with you back hand as well, then your harness lines are too far forward.

However, don't overdo it and move your lines so far back that the mast tries to twist off in front, forcing you to have to pull hard with your front hand to prevent it. The only work either arm should do is make fine trim adjustments or steer. A good general rule is to move the lines back as the wind gets stronger and forward as it gets lighter. If you're having to use your arms to support your weight or balance the rig, then your lines are not correctly adjusted.

In addition to the position of the lines, you should also be adjusting their length to your weight and the conditions. As you get more overpowered, it is important to lengthen your lines so that you can hang back with arms fully extended for maximum leverage. Then when the wind gets lighter, you want to shorten up the lines so that you can keep your arms bent and stay close to the booms. Otherwise you would be leaning too far out and pulling the rig over on top of you. You don't actually have to retie your lines or put on longer or shorter ones. You can get the same effect just by moving the straps closer together or farther apart to position yourself farther from the booms or closer to them.

HOOKING IN AND UNHOOKING

The first time you hook in, it should be on a point of sail somewhere between a close reach and beating. You can effectively use a harness on all points of sail

A

Positioning the Harness Lines

To set your harness lines to the correct position on the booms, first use your hands to determine where the balance point on the boom is by sailing for a few moments. Here, Nancy Johnson is sailing in higher winds *(A)*, and thus her hands are farther back on the booms. The thick arrow indicates the balance point for the booms in these wind conditions, while the thin arrow shows the approximate balance point for sailing in lighter air.

B

C

Once you determine where your hands need to go on the booms, move your harness lines to the same spots *(B,C)*.

The harness line is now properly positioned to share some of the sailing work with your arms *(D)*.

D

Hooking In—Hook Down

A

B

To hook in with the harness hook down (A) first bend your arms to pull yourself and the hook in to the boom and line (B). Don't make the mistake of pulling the boom and line out to you, since you want to be hooking in with your weight balanced more over the board, certainly when you are first learning. Once your weight is in, bend

C

D

your knees to bring the hook down over the line *(C)*. Don't bend at the waist to hook in—you'll lose your leverage and balance. Once hooked in, keep your knees bent to maintain tension on the line so that it won't drop out from the hook. At the same time, extend your arms so that your upper body leans back out *(D)*.

Hooking In—Hook Down (Cont.)

E

F

Extend your legs so that your full weight and leverage are on the line *(E)*. **To unhook,** just bend your arms and arch your torso a little to take your weight off the hook. The line should go slack and fall free *(F)*.

except running, but it is most effective when sailing upwind, where you need the most leverage to support the rig and where your balance is the most stable. As you begin to sail progressively more off the wind, there is progressively less need to hook in to be able to handle the sail and progressively more need for freedom of movement. This doesn't mean that you can't hook in on a reach to give your arms a rest. It just makes it more difficult to move quickly and freely to balance.

Always hook in while sailing. Don't try to luff, hook in, and then trim. With the hook down, you simply bring your weight in, luffing the sail very slightly if you have to maintain leverage, then bend your knees to catch the line with the hook. As soon as you're hooked in, keep your weight on the line and push out so that the tension prevents the line from dropping out of the hook. If you had to luff slightly while hooking in, trim back in as you push out.

Unhooking is easy. All you do is pull yourself up closer to the booms so that there is some slack in the line and it drops out. And if at any time you feel yourself being pulled over by the rig and you need to unhook quickly, just give a sharp jerk on the booms to get close enough for slack to develop and the line to drop out.

To hook in with the hook up, the technique is similar, except that you bend your knees, come in under the line, and then straighten up to catch it with the hook. Since the hook is up, you don't have to worry about keeping tension on the line so it won't fall out. To unhook, just reverse the process, bending at your knees and coming in and out from under the line. And if you are getting pulled over with the hook up, just bend forward at the waist so that the line pulls straight out.

A more advanced technique, either with the hook up or down, is to pull the booms toward you to swing the line up. At the same time, you move your body in to catch the line with the hook. While this might sound a little tricky, it becomes surprisingly easy with just a little practice. The advantage of this technique is that you don't have to bring your weight way in to hook in and therefore don't lose any leverage during the process.

No matter what technique you choose, be sure to practice it enough to feel completely comfortable with it before going on to actually sailing hooked in. At first, just hook in and then unhook, hook in and unhook. These body movements are the key to developing confidence and control while sailing with a harness. Being able to get in and out quickly and easily are also the keys to safe use of a harness.

Hooking In—Hook Up

A

B

To hook in with the hook up *(A)* you have to bend your knees and come in over the board and under the harness line *(B,C).*

C   D

When you straighten up, the line should catch in the hook *(D)*.

E

F

Since the line won't fall out, you can lean back without worrying about maintaining line tension *(E,F)*.

G

H

To unhook, reverse the process of hooking in. First, bend at the knees and move your body in so that you bring the hook out from under the line *(G)*. Then lean out *(H)* so that when you straighten your legs to extend your body you will be clear of the harness line and won't hook in by mistake *(I)*.

I

STEERING, SHEETING, AND BALANCE

Controlling your board, rig, and balance while hooked in is just a matter of coordinating your arms and body with the harness and lines. For any significant changes in direction—for instance from a beat to a reach—you should unhook first. But for minor course adjustments, especially upwind, you can steer while still hooked in by shifting your weight forward and back to move the whole rig forward and back. To make sail trim adjustments, you do the same thing, only you hold the rig stationary while the hook slides along the harness line. In this manner, when you slide your weight forward, the sail is eased out, and when you slide your weight back, the sail is trimmed in further.

Steering While Hooked In

To make small course adjustments while hooked in, shift your whole body and the rig forward or back. Here, Nancy leans forward, bringing the rig forward, which causes the board to steer downwind.

As for balancing, it's all a matter of straightening the legs and leaning back for more leverage, or bending the knees and coming in for less. It's the same theory as when sailing without a harness. To keep from pulling the sail over on top of you, you come back in over the board and transfer the outward pull into downward pull. The only difference is that the pull is with the harness lines instead of the arms. However, if you anticipate having to make any large, quick adjustments to maintain balance, such as in a big set of waves, a wind shift, or a puff or lull, it is best to unhook so that the harness line won't restrict your ability to move in any way.

HOW TO FALL

One of the biggest concerns of people learning to use a harness is falling while hooked in. Actually, falling while using a harness need cause no more problems than falling without one. When you fall in backward while hooked in, you simply keep holding onto the booms just as you normally would to keep from getting hit by the rig. Then when you're in the water, you reach down with one hand, push the line out of the hook, and come out from under the sail. The only time there's any problem at all is when someone panics and tries to get out from under the sail before unhooking. Of course, this just puts tension on the line and makes it that much harder to remove the hook. Just relax. Even move a little closer to the boom so that some slack develops in the line.

It's also important to keep holding onto the boom when you get pulled in by the sail. In fact, you should actually push down on the boom while falling, causing the sail to act like a parachute to give you a soft landing. If you try to resist or end up letting go of the boom, you get jerked over, possibly onto the booms. When either getting pulled in or falling in backward, you can always control your fall and stay out of trouble by holding onto the rig until after you've landed safely in the water.

Balancing While Hooked In

Balancing when hooked in *(A)* is similar to balancing without a harness. Lean back against the lines for increased leverage when the wind is stronger *(B),* and bend your knees and move your weight in over the board for increased stability *(C),* shifting outward pull to downward *(D)* when the wind is lighter. Notice that when you lean back, you can also trim the sail *(B),* and when you move your weight in, you can ease the sail out *(C).*

B

A

C

D

How to Fall When Hooked In

A

B

To avoid being catapulted or thrown against the booms when being overpowered and pulled over by a sail in strong winds *(A)*, keep holding onto the booms *(B)* and push hard against them as you are being pulled over *(C)*. This both slows your fall

C
                                                     D

by filling your sail on the opposite side (turning it into a kind of parachute), and keeps your body away from any harmful contact with the rig when it hits the water *(D)*.

10

Where Do You Go from Here?

Before you can really answer the question of where you go from here with boardsailing, or what you do with what you've learned, it is important first to clarify where you are now, what you've learned, what you know, and what you can do.

After reading this book and practicing the things in it, you should have the knowledge and skills of an intermediate boardsailor able to sail safely upwind and downwind in as much as 12, and maybe even 15, knots of wind. You should know what to look for in a board, a rig, a sailing site, and sailing conditions. You should know what clothing to wear and how to set up your equipment. You should know how to lift the rig with the least amount of effort. You should know how to trim, how to steer, and where to position your feet, hands, and body for different wind strengths and different points of sail. You should know how to tack and jibe and pull the centerboard and save yourself from falling in frontward or backward. You should know how to launch in surf and sail in waves. You should know how to use a harness. You should know how to use your body for leverage and how to maintain balance. You should know the safety and right-of-way rules.

201

Triangle racing, usually around inflatable marks, is an excellent way to hone your boardsailing skills and satisfy that competitive itch.

Granted, knowing how to do all these things is not necessarily the same as actually being able to do them. But even if you are not yet an intermediate boardsailor, you certainly should have the knowledge and ability to become one. All it takes is concentration, patience, and practice, three more things that you should be very familiar with by now.

So this is where you are, your jumping-off point to a whole new world of boardsailing. Think back to the thrill you experienced when you first successfully trimmed the sail and began gliding across the water. That same joy and sense of accomplishment still awaits you as you move on and acquire new skills. This isn't even to say that you have to become an expert or an advanced intermediate to continue to grow as a boardsailor, although many of you will, some by design and determination and others without ever realizing it as it happens. The fact is that boardsailing can be continually fun and challenging no matter what level you choose to sail at. As an intermediate boardsailor, you have the skills and knowledge to explore and learn any number of exciting boardsailing activities.

TRIANGLE RACING

Sailboard racing is an integral part of boardsailing. If you don't believe me, take a closer look at all the "noncompetitive" recreational boardsailors who, as soon as they get near another board, can't help trying to sail faster. Granted, some boardsailors are far more competitive than others, and serious sailboard racers make up only a small portion of the total boardsailing population. But at the same time, for many enthusiasts, racing is a natural extension of one's boardsailing development. It is a means of taking your boardsailing skills to the limit, a way of continually monitoring just how good you really are. And as is the case in many sports, competition generally helps to make you a better recreational boardsailor as well.

It isn't difficult for someone to get into sailboard racing. There is local racing almost all over the country at a level of competition that you need not be an expert to get into. The type of racing you can enter depends, to a certain extent, on the make of board you own. One type of competition is called *one-design racing,* which means that everyone races on the same stock board with the same allowable equipment, so that it is your boardsailing ability alone that determines how well you do. For this reason, one-design racing is extremely popular. However, there are only several makes of sailboards in North America that are numerous enough to provide widespread one-design racing.

If you don't own one of these particular sailboards, your alternative is getting into *open-class racing,* which provides competition for different makes of boards that are similar in size, shape, weight, and sail area. Open-class racing puts more emphasis on the competitiveness of your board and equipment, but the ultimate outcome of a race still depends largely on how well you sail.

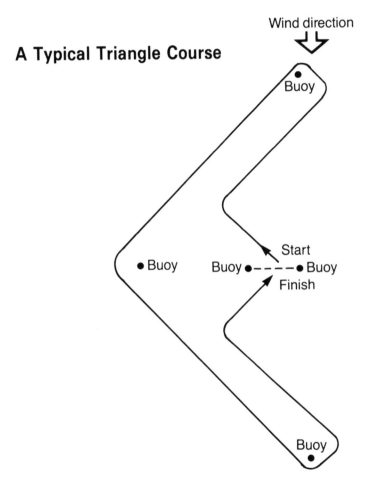

A Typical Triangle Course

A sensible feature of sailboard racing, be it one-design or open-class, is the organization of competitors into weight divisions. Because sailboards are so light in relation to the people sailing them, they are extremely weight sensitive. In other words, the speed and performance of any given board is affected greatly by the weight of the sailor. In fact, if the wind is light to moderate, an experienced but heavy boardsailor will often have trouble keeping up with a less experienced but lighter boardsailor. For this reason, the heavier sailors race against each other and the lighter sailors race against each other, making for competition that is fairer and more fun.

The prospect of entering a sailboard race might seem intimidating to someone who has never raced before and doesn't know the first thing about racing. But with a little preparation, sound intermediate boardsailing skills, and a basic understanding of the format of a race, it needn't be. Races are generally sailed on a triangular course around three buoys set up so that each point of sail is used at some point during the race. Everyone races at one time, starting on the same starting line, sailing around the same buoys, and finishing at the same finish line.

This format makes for some close action, especially at the start and at the buoy roundings, so a good knowledge of the right-of-way rules is essential. In fact, there are a number of additional racing rules that should be learned as soon as possible if you plan to do much racing. A copy of the official racing rules can be bought from the United States Yacht Racing Union, P.O. Box 209, Newport, Rhode Island, 02840, and you can often find some good books that explain the rules at sailboard or sailboat shops.

For the beginning competitor, the start is undoubtedly the most confusing part of a race. To the casual observer, it probably looks as if everybody just mills around with no particular aim other than not running into each other, before roughly lining up and suddenly taking off for the first buoy. The way it actually works is that you start on an imaginary line between two objects, such as a buoy and an anchored boat. The competitors are allowed to maneuver around the starting line to get in a good position so long as they are behind the imaginary line when the starting gun goes off. Guns or horns or whistles are used at intervals to signify how much time is left before the start. This enables you to time your start so that you are as close to the line as possible without being over it when the final gun goes off.

Once you learn the racing rules and understand how the course and start works, you should be capable of entering a sailboard race. You may be a long way from winning a race, but you should at least have all the skills necessary to get around the course in light and moderate winds. It's really nothing more than sail trim, balance, tacking, jibing, beating, reaching, and running—all things that you have learned to do. And those who win are simply those who do these things better than the other competitors. A good attitude to have is

that you are entering a race to learn and to get practice. In this way you will
have fun and get something valuable out of each race no matter where you
finish.

SLALOM RACING

Slalom racing is considered by many to be the most exciting form of sailboard
competition. The format is head-to-head racing against another sailor through
buoys set close enough to each other that tacking and jibing ability becomes
more important than flat-out speed. And slalom racing is not only an excellent
and challenging form of competition, but it is also one of the best ways to
practice boardhandling skills. It's easy to construct and set up the six-buoy
course almost anywhere, enabling you to have informal pickup races with
friends, or sail the course alone to sharpen up your tacking and jibing.

DISTANCE RACING

Distance racing is the marathon of boardsailing. Ranging anywhere from 5
miles to 15 miles in length, a distance race tests endurance and seamanship as
well as the basic sailboard racing skills. The race often begins with a Le Mans
start from the shore and, whenever possible, finishes on shore with a final sprint
across the beach to the finish line. A long-distance race is not beyond an
intermediate boardsailor's abilities as long as he or she is in good shape and can
use a harness. However, it is a good idea to work gradually into distance racing,
starting out with races that aren't too long and are sailed in moderate winds
before racing particularly long distances or in heavy air. Distance racing can
be extremely hard work, but when you finish, regardless of what place you come
in, your reward is a tremendous sense of accomplishment at having made it.
Everyone who finishes is a winner.

The Head Dip

Freestyling

With skill and imagination, you can soon be doing freestyle tricks such as:

Sailing Inside the Booms

The Railride

Tandem Freestyling

The Pirouette

FREESTYLE

Freestyle boardsailing, or to take a term from surfing vocabulary, "hotdog-ging," is a combination of sailing, gymnastics, and dance. It is a natural exten-sion of basic boardsailing skills and maneuvers expressing the freedom of movement that is such an integral part of the sport. Freestyle is for the artist and the showman in all of us. Let's face it, almost everyone likes to show off now and then. It may be a joy in itself to pull off a flashy maneuver, but it's even better if someone happens to be watching.

The novice boardsailor usually does his first trick the first time he saves himself from a fall or performs a tack to jibe with a little extra flair. Beyond that, the average boardsailor is ready to learn some real tricks once he or she has mastered all the different points of sail and can tack, jibe, and turn with confidence and balance. While there are a lot of very advanced freestyle tricks that require a considerable amount of practice and quite a bit of athletic ability, there are also a number of tricks that are well within the ability range of the intermediate boardsailor.

For instance, the first real trick you might learn is a *board 360*, which consists of holding the sail in a stationary, filled position and turning the board in a complete circle underneath it. Another relatively easy trick to pick up is *sailing backward.* Usually done on a run to start with, it also can be done reaching or even beating as you become more expert. Or you can sail *inside the booms,* which entails ducking your head and shoulders through the booms so that you end up leaning back against them to support the rig. Slightly more advanced but still within reach of the average intermediate with some practice are such tricks as *the sail 360,* also called "the helicopter," *sailing from the downwind side, the flare jibe,* which is also an essential racing maneuver, *the tail sink, the head dip,* and the most classic of all boardsailing tricks, *the railride,* in which you actually sail the board on its edge.

The best way to learn tricks is to watch closely some of the better freestyle sailors and then experiment on your own. If you get good enough, you may want to put some of the tricks you've mastered into a routine and enter a freestyle competition, where you sail for two or three minutes and are scored by judges on what tricks you do and how well you do them. Who knows, you may even find you have a real knack for freestyle and eventually end up doing double pirouettes, splits on the rail, and flips through the booms with the best of them.

SHORT-BOARD SAILING

Short-board sailing is a general name I like to use to describe what is commonly known as *wave sailing* or *wave jumping*. These two parts of boardsailing, already immortalized in various soft drink commercials on television, are usually associated with sailing the big surf in Hawaii. With short, light, highly maneuverable boards, expert boardsailors can alternately surf waves with speed and carving ability never imagined by a surfer and launch off the face of waves, turning the sail into a wing and traveling 20 to 30 feet in the air.

But these short boards, which have footstraps to help keep the sailor on the board, two and three fins for tracking and turning ability, and specially cut sails, are by no means limited just to coastal wave sailing. Even on inland lakes, a boardsailor can get out in strong winds and carve high-speed turns or catch air off of one-foot chop. High wind is really the common denominator for short boards, whether they are sailed in big waves or on relatively flat water. Still another term, coined by the Europeans for this type of board, is fun board.

Because these boards are shorter, they have less flotation and are therefore more difficult to balance on. Actually, short boards are divided into three categories according to length, flotation, and stability. Boards that are about 10 or 11 feet long are relatively stable and are called *floaters*. Because they are the most stable, they are a good entry-level board for aspiring short-board sailors. They sometimes even come with small, retractable centerboards to afford upwind ability that most short boards lack.

At the other end of the scale are *sinkers*, which usually run 7 or 8 feet. Sinkers get their name from the fact that they are so small and light and have so little flotation that they actually sink under the weight of the sailor unless they are moving at a certain minimum speed. This means that you can't tack a sinker, since you lose too much speed in the process. Instead, you learn to turn by carving high-speed jibes. The lack of flotation also means that you cannot stand on a sinker to pull up the rig. To get going, you use something called a *water start*. This involves getting the rig just a little up into the wind and then using the strength of the wind in the sail to actually lift you up onto the board and get you sailing immediately. It's a little like the technique for launching off a beach in waves, only you are lying in the water instead of standing. Obviously, this all means you have to have fairly strong winds before you can even think about taking a sinker out.

Whether on waves or flat water, short boards are for sailing in high wind.

Somewhere in between the sinker and the floater is a category of short board called a *semi-floater,* which draws a compromise between the performance of a sinker and the stability of a floater. Most advanced intermediates, as long as they are not too heavy, should be able to tack and rope start a semi-floater, although it takes some careful balancing.

The main point about these three categories is that there are short boards available for all ability levels above beginner. The intermediate can start out

with a floater, learn all the techniques of high wind and wave sailing, and then move up to a semi-floater—and eventually maybe even a sinker.

One word of caution concerning short boards. The shorter the board and the less the flotation, the more difficult it is to sail upwind. So the intermediate just getting into short-board sailing should be careful not to get too far downwind. Getting back can be a long and arduous task.

AND BEYOND

The important thing about short boards or freestyle, or distance racing, slalom, or triangle racing, is that they are all ways of enjoying the sport of boardsailing. But don't make the mistake of thinking that it is the activity alone that makes boardsailing fun. The element that is common to all of these boardsailing activities is that you are sailing and learning, and improving and exercising your body and your mind. And no matter how much you learn about boardsailing or how good you get or how many ways you find to enjoy the sport, there is always something new to learn, there is always room for improvement, and there are always new ways, new settings, and new people with whom to discover the beauty, challenge, and joy of boardsailing over and over again.

See you on the water.

"See you on the water."

Glossary

ABS Plastic: A popular construction material for the outer shell on sailboards, stiffer than polyethylene, but softer than epoxy, the two other most popular construction materials.

Backing the Sail: Trimming the sail on the back side, either to use it as a brake to stop the board in the water or to help pivot the board and turn faster.

Batten: A long, flat, thin piece of semi-stiff material inserted into pockets in the back of the sail to help support it and give it shape, and prevent it from fluttering in strong winds.

Beam Reach: Point of sail in which the board is sailing at a 90° angle to the wind.

Beating: Point of sail at which the board is sailing as close into the wind as possible—approximately 45 degrees to the wind. See "closehauled."

Beaufort Scale: A scale that measures and describes wind strength in terms of Forces 1 through 10, each Force representing an increased speed range in miles per hour.

Board: The hull portion of a sailboard, made of various flotation materials, which supports the rig and the boardsailor.

Boardsailing Shoes: Specially designed shoes that provide increased traction and footing on the wet surface of a sailboard.

Board 360: A freestyle trick in which the board is spun in a complete circle beneath the stationary rig.

Booms: The pair of lightweight curved bars joined together at both ends and curved to form an ellipse that holds the sail out from the mast and that the boardsailor grasps to support and control the sail. Also called "wishbones."

Broad Reaching: The point of sail at which the wind is coming partially from behind the board and partially from the side. Halfway between a beam reach and running.

Centerboard: A piece of equipment that fits through a slot in the board and inhibits sideslipping when sailing. There are three basic types of centerboards: daggerboards, kickup centerboards, and fully retractable centerboards.

Centerboard Slot: An opening cut in the board through which the centerboard is inserted into the water.

Centerline: An imaginary balance line running down the middle of the board from nose to tail and passing through the centerboard slot and the mast hole.

Closehauled: Point of sail at which the sailboard is sailing as close into the wind as possible, approximately 45 degrees. See "beating."

Close Reaching: Point of sail at which the wind is coming partially from in front of the board and partially from the side. Halfway between beating and a beam reach.

Crest: The peak, or highest point of a wave.

Daggerboard: Type of centerboard that can only be raised straight up or down in the centerboard slot.

Distance Racing: Boardsailing version of a marathon.

Downhaul: A piece of line that attaches the forward bottom corner of the sail to the top of the universal and helps to adjust the shape of the sail.

Downwind: Away from the wind. Also, that side or direction the wind is blowing toward.

Drake, Jim: Co-inventor of the first sailboard.

Farmer John: A style of wetsuit that covers the legs and torso, but leaves the arms and shoulders exposed.

Fathead: A type of sail, used mostly with highwind sailboards, with increased sail area at the top supported by a full-length batten.

Fiberglass: The stiffest construction material used in sailboards, found mostly in custom-made highwind models.

Flare Jibe: A quick jibe in which the tail of the board is momentarily sunk and the board is spun around. See "jibing."

Floater: Any board that fully supports the weight of the boardsailor even when motionless in the water.

Footstraps: Straps attached to the top of highwind boards into which a boardsailor inserts his feet so that he can stay on the board in waves and at high speeds.

Freestyle: The art of trick boardsailing or hotdogging. Incorporates imaginative maneuvers with the board, rig, and body, either for fun or in competition.

Full-Displacement Board: A sailboard with an extremely round bottom from nose to tail, designed for use upwind and in light air.

Full-Size Sail: A large sail designed to provide sufficient power and performance for intermediate to experienced boardsailors in moderate to strong winds. It is usually unsuitable for learning or for very high winds.

Fully-Retractable Centerboard: A type of centerboard that can be pivoted flush into a slot in the bottom of the board when not needed.

Funboard: Term coined by Europeans for a board with footstraps and a fully retractable centerboard designed for high speed reaching.

Harness: A brief vest with a hook attached to the front which allows the wearer to connect himself to the booms by means of harness lines and which takes the strain of supporting the rig off the arms.

Harness Lines: Lines attached to the booms which the boardsailor catches on his harness hook to reduce the strain of the sail on his arms.

Head Dip: A freestyle trick in which the boardsailor leans over backwards and dips his or her head in the water.

Helicopter: A freestyle trick in which the boardsailor and rig do a complete turn on the board while it sails a constant course.

High-Performance: Any piece of equipment or any technique relating to the upper levels of speed and maneuverability.

Highwind Centerboard: A small centerboard, usually swept back toward the tail, which reduces the board's tendency to round up or rail at high speeds.

Hooking In: The process of catching the harness lines on the harness hook.

Hypothermia: A state, caused by cold water, wind chill, and physical exertion, in which the body temperature falls below 35 degrees centigrade, producing loss of coordination and consciousness, and even death.

Inhaul: The piece of line which ties the front of the booms to the mast.

Jibing: A turn away from the wind which finishes with the wind blowing on the opposite side of the sail from when the turn started.

Kickup Centerboard: A type of centerboard that can be pivoted back and up against the bottom of the board so that it protrudes less far into the water.

Leach: The back edge of a sail.

Learning Board: A wide, buoyant, stable board specifically designed for beginners.

Leash: The most important piece of safety equipment on a sailboard. A piece of line that attaches the rig to the board so that the board cannot break loose and be carried away from the boardsailor.

Luffing: The flapping of the sail when the wind gets on the back side of it caused by the sail not being trimmed in far enough or the board being sailed too much into the wind.

Lull: A momentary decrease in wind strength or wave size.

Marginal Sail: A sail slightly smaller than full size, used for teaching or for sailing in stronger winds where the boardsailor would be overpowered by a larger sail.

Mast: Pole made of fiberglass or aluminum and inserted into a sleeve on the front edge of the sail to support the sail in the wind.

Mast Hole: Hole in the board into which the bottom of the universal is inserted, attaching the mast to the board.

Midpoint Line: The balance line on a board between the nose and the tail, usually located somewhere between the mast hole and the centerboard slot.

Non-Skid: Roughened, textured, or patterned surface on the top of the board to give the boardsailor better footing.

Nose: The front of the board.

Offshore Wind: Any wind that is blowing from land and toward the water. Potentially dangerous because of its ability to blow a boardsailor away from shore.

Offwind: Any course that heads across or at any angle away from the wind. See "beam reaching," "broad reaching," and "running."

One-Design Racing: Any racing where all the boards are of identical design and sail size.

Onshore Wind: Any wind that blows from off the water toward land.

Open Class Racing: Racing in which the competitors are allowed to use boards of varying designs as long as they are within certain measurement parameters and the sails do not exceed given size restrictions.

Outhaul: Piece of line that attaches the rear lower corner of the sail to the back of the booms and helps to adjust the shape of the sail.

Overtrimming: The act of pulling the sail in beyond its most efficient angle to the wind, causing reduced speed and increased sideslipping through the water.

Planing: The point when a board travels fast enough to break free of the water and skim across the top of it at even greater speeds.

Points of Sail: Different angles to the wind, and thus different directions, that a board can sail. See "beam reach," "beating," "close reaching," "reaching," "broad reaching," and "running."

Polyethylene: Plastic material used for the outer shell in sailboard construction.

Port: Nautical term for "left."

Prevailing Wind: Predominant wind direction and strength in a given locale at a given time of year or day.

Pulling the Centerboard: Removing the centerboard from its slot in the board and carrying it over your arm by the handle to gain stability when sailing downwind in heavy air.

Racing Board: Any board that is used for racing; or a board designed specifically for racing performance rather than general recreational sailing.

Rail: The sides, or edges of a sailboard.

Railing: Putting one rail or the other down into the water either purposely to help steer the board, or by accident when out of control.

Rail Ride: The act of sailing the board on its edge or rail. When planned by an experienced boardsailor, it is a freestyle trick. When the result of the centerboard hydroplaning to the surface at high speed, the prelude to a swim.

Reaching: Point of sail in which the wind is coming just forward of the beam, or even with, or slightly behind, it.

Ready Position: Stationary position, preparatory to trimming and actually sailing, in which the boardsailor holds the sail up and lets it luff in the wind.

Rig: The mast, sail, booms, and the lines that hold them together—basically, everything above the board.

Right-of-Way Rules: Rules of the road that delineate vessels' responsibilities for avoiding collisions when sailing and/or other craft meet. More extensive rules also cover racing situations.

Rope Turn: Any turn, including a "rope tack" or a "rope jibe," in which the boardsailor holds onto the uphaul and tilts the rig to turn the board while the sail is luffing. The first type of turn taught to beginners.

Rounding Up: The act of the board turning up into the wind. Often accidentally experienced by beginners if the sail is not trimmed correctly.

Running: Point of sail in which the wind is coming directly from behind the board.

Sail: Triangular piece of synthetic cloth supported by the mast and booms which catches the wind's power in order to move the board through the water.

Sailboard: The correct generic term for a surfboard with a sail, used instead of "windsurfer," the brand name of the first sailboard.

Sailing Backwards: A freestyle trick in which the boardsailor stands and trims the sail from the nose side of the mast and sails the board tailfirst.

Sailing from the Downwind Side: A freestyle trick in which the boardsailor stands on the board's leeward side (the side farthest from the wind) and trims the sail by pushing on the booms instead of pulling on them from the upwind side.

Sail 360: Same as a "helicopter."

Schweitzer, Hoyle: Co-inventor of the first sailboard and primary promoter of the sport of boardsailing.

Semi-Displacement Board: A board which has a rounded bottom forward, but a flat, planing surface back by the tail.

Semi-Floater: A board, usually of the highwind variety, between 9 and 11 feet, that performs best in strong winds, but will float the weight of most boardsailors even when stationary.

Sheeting: Adjusting the angle of the sail to the wind. Taken from the sailing term, "sheet"—a line on a sailboat used to trim a sail. See "trimming."

Shortie: A wetsuit style that covers the torso and upper legs, but leaves the arms, shoulders, and lower legs exposed.

Sinker: A highwind board, usually 7 to 9 feet long, that will perform only in 15 knots of wind or more and cannot float the weight of the boardsailor unless it is moving fast through the water.

Skeg: A small underwater protrusion, or fin, at the tail of a sailboard which provides steering stability.

Slalom Racing: A form of head-to-head competition between two boardsailors that requires fast maneuvering through a close course of six buoys.

Starboard: Nautical term for "right."

Stationary Turn: A turn done with the uphaul but without the board sailing forward. Same as a "rope turn."

Storm Sail: A very small sail that allows a boardsailor to go out in winds that would overpower him if he were using a larger marginal sail or a full-size sail.

Tacking: Turning through the wind such that it ends up blowing on the opposite side of the sail.

Tail: The back end of a sailboard.

Tail Sink: A freestyle trick in which the boardsailor steps to the tail of the board and lifts the nose high out of the water while still sailing.

Tether: A learning aid consisting of about 100 feet of light line, one end of which is attached to the sailboard, the other secured to a buoy or anchor, or held by a friend to prevent excessive drifting—and thus paddling—while learning to sail.

Triangle Racing: Racing done around three buoys so that the boardsailor's skill on each point of sail is challenged. Also called "course racing" or "Olympic racing."

Trimming: Pulling in on the booms with the back hand to fill the sail with wind and start sailing. Also, simply adjusting the angle of the sail to the wind so that it stops luffing. See "sheeting."

Trough: The lowest part of a wave, or the low point, or valley, between two waves.

Undertrimming: Not pulling the sail in far enough, so that it luffs and spills wind rather than catching and holding it.

Unhooking: Removing the harness lines from the harness hook so that the boardsailor is supporting the rig only with his arms.

Universal Joint: The connector between the board and the mast which allows the rig to be moved in any direction or plane. One of the unique features that distinguishes a sailboard from a sailboat.

Uphaul: A piece of thick line tied to the front of the booms where they attach to the mast and used by the boardsailor to pull the rig to an upright position.

Uphaul Bungie: A piece of elastic shock cord attached to the end of the uphaul and to the top of the universal that keeps the uphaul out of the way when sailing, but allows easy retrieval for pulling up the rig.

Upwind: Toward the wind, or close to the side or direction the wind is blowing from.

Vest: A kind of wetsuit; essentially a neoprene jacket without sleeves.

Water Start: A method of raising the rig out of the water and starting to sail in which the boardsailor, while still in the water, holds the trimmed sail up into the wind and lets it lift him up onto the board. A water start works only in high winds and is a necessary technique for sailing sinkers.

Wave Sailing, Wave Jumping: Sailing done in breaking waves, usually on highwind boards, in which the board surfs on the waves when moving with them and hurtles off the waves when sailing against them.

Wetsuit: A neoprene rubber suit made in various styles to cover the body to varying degrees and to keep it warm by trapping a thin layer of water which the body itself heats.

White Water: Turbulent water left after a wave has broken.

Windsurfer: The brand name of the original sailboard invented by Hoyle Schweitzer and Jim Drake. Still the largest class of sailboard in the world today.

Wishbone Booms: See "booms."

The Beaufort Scale

Named after Sir Francis Beaufort, who developed it, the Beaufort Scale indicates wind force by a series of numbers from 0 to 17. You can learn to gauge wind speeds by observing the effect of the wind on water and land, as charted below.

Beaufort (Force) Number	MPH	Knots	Name	Appearance of land and water
0	Under 1	Under 1	Calm	Smoke rises vertically; water calm, mirrorlike
1	1–3	1–3	Light air	Wind direction shown by smoke but not by weathervanes; ripples on water
2	4–7	4–6	Light breeze	Leaves rustle; wind felt on face; weathervanes moved by wind; small wavelets on water
3	8–12	7–10	Gentle breeze	Leaves and twigs in constant motion; wind causes flags to flutter; large wavelets, scattered whitecaps on water
4	13–18	11–16	Moderate breeze	Wind raises dust and loose paper; small branches are moved; small waves, many whitecaps on water
5	19–24	17–21	Fresh breeze	Small leafed trees begin to sway; moderate waves, whitecaps, some spray on water
6	25–31	22–27	Strong breeze	Large branches in motion; phone lines whistle; umbrellas used with difficulty; large waves, whitecaps everywhere, spray on water
7	32–38	28–33	Moderate gale	Whole trees in motion; difficult to walk against wind; sea heaps, white foam blows in streaks
8	39–46	34–40	Fresh gale	Wind breaks twigs off trees; walking impeded; waves long with well-marked white streaks on surface
9	47–54	41–47	Strong gale	Slight structural damage to buildings occurs; shingles torn off roofs; high waves, rolling seas, streaks everywhere, reduced visibility due to heavy spray
10	55–63	48–55	Whole gale	Trees uprooted; considerable structural damage to buildings; extremely high waves with overhanging crests; reduced visibility
11	64–72	56–64	Storm	Widespread damage; find secure shelter!
12–17			Hurricane	Devastation